Children

Experiences

of

Classrooms

Sara Miller McCune founded SAGE Publishing in 1965 to support the dissemination of usable knowledge and educate a global community. SAGE publishes more than 1000 journals and over 800 new books each year, spanning a wide range of subject areas. Our growing selection of library products includes archives, data, case studies and video. SAGE remains majority owned by our founder and after her lifetime will become owned by a charitable trust that secures the company's continued independence.

Los Angeles | London | New Delhi | Singapore | Washington DC | Melbourne

Children's Experiences of Classrooms

of

Talking about being pupils in the classroom.

Eleanore Hargreaves

Los Angeles | London | New Delhi
Singapore | Washington DC | Melbourne

Los Angeles | London | New Delhi
Singapore | Washington DC | Melbourne

SAGE Publications Ltd
1 Oliver's Yard
55 City Road
London EC1Y 1SP

SAGE Publications Inc.
2455 Teller Road
Thousand Oaks, California 91320

SAGE Publications India Pvt Ltd
B 1/I 1 Mohan Cooperative Industrial Area
Mathura Road
New Delhi 110 044

SAGE Publications Asia-Pacific Pte Ltd
3 Church Street
#10-04 Samsung Hub
Singapore 049483

Editor: Marianne Lagrange
Editorial assistant: Robert Patterson
Production editor: Nicola Marshall
Copyeditor: Solveig Gardner Servian
Proofreader: Derek Markham
Indexer: Silvia Benvenuto
Marketing manager: Dilhara Attygalle
Cover design: Sheila Tong
Typeset by: C&M Digitals (P) Ltd, Chennai, India
Printed by: CPI Group (UK) Ltd, Croydon, CR0 4YY

© Eleanore Hargreaves 2017

First published 2017

Apart from any fair dealing for the purposes of research or
private study, or criticism or review, as permitted under the
Copyright, Designs and Patents Act, 1988, this publication
may be reproduced, stored or transmitted in any form, or
by any means, only with the prior permission in writing of
the publishers, or in the case of reprographic reproduction,
in accordance with the terms of licences issued by
the Copyright Licensing Agency. Enquiries concerning
reproduction outside those terms should be sent to
the publishers.

Library of Congress Control Number: 2016951406

British Library Cataloguing in Publication data

A catalogue record for this book is available from
the British Library

ISBN 978-1-4739-5716-9
ISBN 978-1-4739-5717-6 (pbk)

At SAGE we take sustainability seriously. Most of our products are printed in the UK using FSC papers and boards.
When we print overseas we ensure sustainable papers are used as measured by the PREPS grading system.
We undertake an annual audit to monitor our sustainability.

To Jasmine and Wesley:

My children, my teachers

Contents

List of Figures   x
About the Author   xi
Foreword   xii
Acknowledgements   xiv

Introduction: what this book is about   1

Children's experiences of classrooms: talking about being
pupils in the classroom   1
Children's experiences of classrooms: outline of the book   4
The original research projects referred to in this book   8

1 Children's experiences of classrooms: why they matter   10

Four reasons why it is valuable to listen to children's words   10
Pupils' perceptions are different from adults'   15
Children's classroom learning: a cognitive, affective, social
and physical experience?   17
A focus on the classroom emphasises each pupil's experience   20
Schiro's purposes for schooling: the effective classroom is one
that achieves its purpose   20

2 Authority and authoritarianism in the classroom   23

The potentially restrictive influence of authoritarianism in
classrooms around the world   25
Children's words: how the dominant teacher's stress or anger
could be experienced by children in the classroom   28
The structures of authoritarian classrooms   30
Children's words: the link between the authoritarian
classroom and children's fear   31
Children's words: children's classroom fears in a country ridden
with fear   36
Defining authority in the classroom: when legitimate authority
becomes coercive authoritarianism   40

Why authoritarianism?   43
Children's words: children's 'tricks' in classrooms as a way of
combating an authoritarian culture   44
Freedom versus prescription in the classroom   48
Activities for classroom practice   50

3 Autonomy in the classroom   **51**

Autonomy   52
Children's words: pupils' critical inquiry and comment   59
Metalearning is the key to autonomy   61
Children's words: making use of metalearning to combat fear   63
Relatedness to peers and teacher and the link to autonomy   66
Children's words: how relatedness supported autonomy   67
Children's words: how collaborative group learning supported
autonomy more effectively than the traditional classroom   69
Children's words: children making choices in the classroom
increased their autonomous engagement   73
Children's words: pupils experienced that autonomously choosing
talk-partners supported their engagement, enjoyment and
metalearning capacity   77
Activities for classroom practice   80

4 Teacher feedback in the classroom   **81**

The traditional definition of 'feedback'   81
Divergent and process-focused feedback   82
Feedback focusing on the self   84
Children's words: what pupils said about teacher feedback   87
Children's words: teacher feedback across a whole literacy lesson
where the teacher's purposes were at odds with pupils'   93
Children's words: young children critiqued the teacher's overly
directive feedback   98
Activities for classroom practice   104

5 Social class in the classroom   **105**

Social disadvantage and schooling: a segregated system   105
Definitions of 'working class'   107
Middle-class views of working-class pupils   108
Classroom influences on pupils' experience of the classroom   110
Children's words: working-class pupils noticed the teacher's
differentiated treatment according to social class   111
The links between social class and 'ability' groups in classrooms   113
Children's words: 'ability' grouping was okay for those at the top
but even hard work did not get pupils into the top groups   115

Schiro's first purpose for schooling and its relationship to
cultural capital as played out in the classroom   120
Schiro's further purposes for schooling: have these been met in
relation to working-class pupils?   122
Children's words: transformation occurred through the reading
and writing of the Freedom Writers   122
Valuing pupils for what they are: transformation at
St George-in-the-East secondary modern school   124
Activities for teachers   125

References   127
Index   134

List of Figures

0.1   The responsive teacher, drawing by year 5 pupil   1

1.1   The traditional classroom, picture by year 5 pupil   12

2.1   'The teacher's like, really, really big!' Picture by year 5 pupil   23
2.2   The scary teacher, drawn by year 5 pupils   38

3.1   The metalearning cycle of active learning   62
3.2   CGL learning set, drawn by year 5 pupil   70

About the Author

Eleanore Hargreaves is Reader in Learning and Pedagogy at the UCL Institute of Education, London UK, where she has worked since 1995. Her key research interest has always been learning, especially how young children learn and experience learning. She began her career at the Institute of Education as a researcher for an ESRC-funded project that led to the co-authored book, *What makes a good primary school teacher?* (Gipps, McCallum and Hargreaves, 2000) in which assessment and feedback strategies in primary classrooms were described. This led to Eleanore's ongoing interest in feedback and its wider implications for children's learning experiences, reflected in her own project investigating feedback in primary classrooms in 2010–12. Her early work on learning was contextualised within the framework of Assessment for Learning although more recent research has focused more on pupils' affective experiences of classroom learning, including their feelings of fear. In 2015 she co-edited *The SAGE handbook of learning* with David Scott.

Eleanore has a long-standing connection with Alexandria in Egypt and her most recent work has been exploring how children experience language learning in this very different social context. She has also carried out consultancy work in Hong Kong, India, Macedonia, Pakistan, Qatar, Somalia and Saudi Arabia. Eleanore has two children who have inspired much of her work with pupils in classrooms.

Foreword

Chris Watkins, University of London Institute of Education

Experiencing classrooms

Before you read on, this foreword invites you to recall. I can confidently assume that you have experienced classrooms as a pupil, so what happens when you recall those experiences? Do special occasions inform your memory? If so, what is it about them that made them special? And what is it that characterises your ordinary experience of classrooms (if your memory and vocabulary allow)? Might there be aspects that are not part of your memory – because they were not a focus of attention at the time?

Do you recall anyone ever asking you about your experience of the classroom? And I do not mean the ritual 'How was school today?' 'Okay' (end of conversation). I safely predict that your answer is 'No', since even large-scale research projects do not do it. This state of affairs means that the key element in human learning is missing – the learner's perception of their activity, its context and their learning.

Eleanore, with her considerable background in this field, has collected a range of studies that utilise rich and significant conversations with learners in classrooms about their experience. It is a focus which has been sadly missing. This is reflected, for example, in a UK web-search for 'Children's experiences in classrooms', which gives five results (four of them a report on one nursery). And a UK web-search for 'Children's experiences of classrooms' gives zero results.

The classroom has been shown to be a key influence on learning, but pupils' voice has been omitted. Some research has focused on the importance of the classroom but still continues to NOT ask pupils about the experience. The United Nations Convention on the Rights of the Child states that children have a right to have their voice heard in judicial proceedings – but a parallel does not exist in classrooms.

There's no situation that's quite like a classroom. It's one of the most crowded situations on the face of the planet, and one of the busiest – teachers can be involved in a thousand interactions a day. And pupils spend more waking hours in a classroom than they do at home. But the uniqueness of classrooms is not always a valuable specialty. The dominant patterns in classrooms could be unique and not helpful.

After four decades of studies of classroom learning issues using hidden microphones and video cameras, Nuthall's previous book was given the title *The Hidden Lives of Learners* (2007). Now this book helps us make the hidden visible. A key focus on pupil participation and learner voice is evident in the best programmes that focus on learning.

This book's chapters address key issues of classrooms: pupil autonomy, competence and relatedness. These are greatly related: 'The higher the perceived quality of relatedness, the greater one's feelings of autonomy and competence.'

Classrooms are surprisingly similar across the differing country cultures of our world. This book accesses a rich range of countries. And the international comparisons beyond this book show that the countries that achieve best performance, Finland and Singapore, are those which focus on learning.

Read on for inspiring, challenging and constructive voices on the current state of classrooms and how to improve them. I confidently assume that readers of this book will be adults, perhaps teachers. In which case please ask pupils you know: 'What are your best classroom experiences? How did they happen? How can we create more?' This will start the process of transformation.

Suggested reading

NICHD Early Child Care Research Network (2005). A Day in Third Grade: A Large-Scale Study of Classroom Quality and Teacher and Student Behavior. *Elementary School Journal*, 105 (3), 305–323.

Nuthall, G. (2007). *The hidden lives of learners*. Wellington: NZCER.

Robinson, C. (2014). *Children, their voices and their experiences of school: what does the evidence tell us?* York: Cambridge Primary Review Trust.

Ryan, R.M. (1995). Psychological Needs and the Facilitation of Integrative Processes. *Journal of Personality* 63 (3), 397–427.

Wall, K. (2012). 'It Wasn't Too Easy, Which Is Good If You Want To Learn': An Exploration of Pupil Participation and Learning to Learn. *Curriculum Journal*, 23 (3), 283–305.

Acknowledgements

I would like to thank heartily the following people who helped me to write this book:

Chris Watkins, my mentor for 20 years but of particular support in the final stages of writing this book; pupils Millie, Freya, Mo, Eloise, Lucy, Jed, Alex, Daniel, William; Krystyna Scipior and Erik Starkie; Gordon Stobart; Rebecca Vaughan; Serena Beasley; Alison Hinton-Childs and all the participating pupils at their school; the girls and boys who participated in the research in Ramallah, their teachers and Saida Affouneh; children and teachers in the nine classes in Alexandria; my dream team there, Mohamed Mahgoub and Dalia Elhawary; British Council ELTRA for funding that research; Indy Staples; and the following MA researchers and the pupils they carried research out with: Jon Filer, Rob Gratton, Sean Macnamara, Laura Quick, Luke Rolls, Christine Yeomans, Shivani Garg, Shaima Haroon, Hugh Heneghan, Konstantia Karvela, Wan Ju, and Yei Je Son. And finally, thank you to Jasmine for helping me with the references and thank you to Wesley and Tim for their lively encouragement.

Introduction: what this book is about

Figure 0.1   The responsive teacher, drawing by year 5 pupil (Hargreaves et al., 2016)

Children's experiences of classrooms: talking about being pupils in the classroom

The children's words cited in this book suggest that children can tell us a great deal about how children experience classrooms, experiences that as teachers we may not have known about before. The fact that pupils experience the classroom *differently* from teachers has kept appearing as a theme in the children's words in this book. Because the role of the teacher is so different from the role of the pupil, this difference is not surprising. However, it is an important reason consciously to ask pupils how they are finding the classroom – and to take their words as authoritative. As Kenny said to his teachers (see Chapter 5), 'You don't need to love us. All you need to do is treat us like humans'. The request is to treat pupils like humans rather than like 'herds of an identical animal' which have little valuable to say and cannot take mature, responsible decisions. The words of the children in this book show that children do not need to be silent in the classroom. Silencing belongs to the traditional conception of learning – as listening and absorbing. However, by turning the power balance around and by we teachers listening instead to children's words, the child steps into a self who becomes capable of more than listening and absorbing. At the same time, more purposes can be achieved if children learn in autonomous ways. Then the whole picture looks different. As suggested in Chapter 2, the authoritative (*not* the authori*tarian*) teacher aims to distribute knowledge in order to support pupils to construct their own knowledge and make meaning from it. The authoritative teacher does so because s/he wants the pupils to flourish as people and to learn skills and knowledge about valuable aspects of life through the curriculum.

I think that the word 'distribute' is important here. Ann Brown and colleagues (1993) coined the classroom term 'distributed expertise'. The shift in emphasis that many of the children's words in this book seem to advise is a shift towards more distributed authority in the classroom: more distributed knowledge-construction, distributed meaning-making, distributed assessment, distributed decision making, distributed respect and distributed care. This implies a classroom where negotiation guides action rather than telling; where democracy is the baseline rather than autocracy.

A key way recommended by the children in this book of distributing authority within the classroom is through children participating in deciding what is learnt and how it is learnt (Chapter 3). This choice appears to be crucial for them to develop a flourishing sense of self as a valuable and respected person. It also helps nurture a capacity for critical comment which will build up a potential future society full of adults with a rich capacity for responsible critique and decision making. The evidence is that without pupils' buy-in, dominance of the teacher's values and rules may serve only to alienate pupils (Chapter 2). This appears to be a particularly crucial issue for working-class pupils whose voices may be the most often squeezed out of the decision-making process. All pupils may need to be helped to make choices and decisions and not given too many, but they clearly appreciate very much the chance to air their views about classroom issues that affect their experiences and learning. Sara summed it up (Chapter 1), saying that she was very joyful because this was 'the first time someone has come into our classroom and asked me my opinion'. The irony is that by asking pupils to comment on learning content and learning arrangements, this helps them to construct knowledge and to make meaning (i.e. to learn) as well as helping them to develop a sense of self. It is what can be called a 'win-win situation'. It is, however, not always easy to negotiate classroom arrangements within the kind of school where an atmosphere of social judgement dominates, where both teachers and children feel continuously judged by others.

It is striking, though, that the words of children in this book do indicate the power of their authority. Sometimes they show extraordinary insight. Their words often seem surprisingly wise and remind us how insightful even the youngest child may be about the way things are. Drawing on their wise words seems to be a safe way for distributing authority within the classroom. Instead of the traditional 'talk and chalk' by the teacher, pupils can engage in carefully orchestrated dialogue among each other and with the teacher, for example in learning sets of six (Chapter 3). Such dialogue may address how the class operates or may concern a domain topic. Either way, every person is valued as both expert and as novice. What becomes clear is that when children themselves put thoughts into spoken words, as Vygotsky explained, this helps them to clarify those thoughts for themselves. When they then have to distribute those ideas to others in the class (i.e. explain or teach them) an even deeper understanding can come about. Having the right atmosphere of support in the classroom is of course a prerequisite for the success of this approach of distributed authority.

What also comes through the words of children in a crystal clear way is that the classroom for them is not just a place to get information. Their experience of the classroom is distributed across their affective, social and physical aspects, not just their cognitive capacities. Even if a particular teacher believes that learning is just about getting information, pupils are meanwhile having strong feelings in this same teacher's classroom. They feel the teacher's moods and glances and care passionately about their own relationship with the teacher in the classroom as well as their relationships with other children. Children also report being affected by the physical environment of the classroom, including how the desks are arranged and how they are grouped. They show, too, that they are aware of the wider social contexts of their classrooms, readily picking up messages about their status in the classroom or in society more widely. This appears to be true even for very young children (Chapter 4). However much we as teachers focus on the cognitive in learning, pupils will continue to distribute their focus across the cognitive, affective, social and physical aspects of learning as these are all important dimensions of their actual experiences in the classroom.

Another feature of distributed learning in the classroom relates to how differently each child responds to the same classroom situation. Among a classroom of pupils there are many different backgrounds, attitudes, ways of responding, ways of relating, ideas and capacities. The children in Emerald Primary School (Chapter 4), for example, stressed the importance of the teacher giving each child pupil-specific appropriate feedback. The scenario with Vijay and Laila illustrates how two children struggled in very different ways from each other, despite both being in the same 'bottom ability' group. In this class too, it is noted that the teacher used autonomy-promoting feedback more with 'higher' groups than with 'lower' groups, as if 'ability' grouping meant that all pupils in an 'ability' group shared the same capacity for proactive engagement and self-direction. This reinforces the reasons for listening to every child's voice in the classroom, in order to allow the teacher to distribute her/his attentions appropriately and equitably. This could be likened to pure democracy, where not only the majority are served but minorities are protected and nurtured too.

It is up to each teacher, parent or other educator to decide which ways they believe are most valuable towards the aim of becoming increasingly responsive to each child's individual existence and open to their dynamic and unpredictable development (see Saevi, 2015).

Children's experiences of classrooms: outline of the book

Mariam in year 5 wrote for the research team some insights about classroom learning and teaching (Hargreaves et al., 2016). She added:

> I am very hopeful that someone will read this and know what I need and the way I want to learn. I hope you don't throw my [response] paper away and say it's child's talk. Please take what I say seriously as I am hoping that education will improve. This is the first time someone has listened to what I would like to say. (Mariam, year 5)

It is the aim of this book to look inside the classroom and take very seriously the insights of children like Mariam. The book explores what several children have said about their current and past experiences in the classroom and investigates their interpretations of these. I aim in this book to showcase how authoritative and insightful children's comments can be. I also hope to emphasise how an educator's investigation of children's perspectives and feelings can actually make teaching more effective for a range of purposes – as well as potentially more fulfilling for the teacher.

Children's experiences of authority and authoritarianism in the classroom

Clive Harber (2015) summed up one of the key findings of this book:

> As a teacher I possess tremendous power to make a child's life miserable or joyous. I can be a tool of torture or an instrument of inspiration. (p.243)

This realisation rings true when listening to children talk about their teachers' anger in the classroom which seemed to control them with emotional intensity. The angry or shouting teacher could freeze them with fear or fuel them with anger. Chapter 2 portrays how the teacher was dominant traditionally because s/he was the only one with the knowledge. Now the teacher's dominance has continued as a legacy into the 21st century, even though educators understand that knowledge transmission is only one small part of the teacher's job today. This archaic model of pupil dependence and teacher dominance (in many cases spread across the world by British colonialists in the 19th century) seems to penetrate all the far-flung places represented in this book. Children's voices from England, Ireland, Australia, Egypt and Palestine, and from as far afield as Korea and Taiwan, make a very clear link between these traditional authoritarian classrooms and pupils' experiences of fear and anger. The pupils who were interviewed at Meadowbank School in England, for example, described feeling fear in the classroom which interrupted their concentration and silenced their voices.

Worryingly, the children from Meadowbank School had teachers who particularly aimed to promote their autonomy. Yet despite that aim, the traditional relationship lingered, of dominance by the teacher and dependence by the child. Pupils there were scared of teachers when they shouted or punished them and were scared of their head teacher and the deputy head. This led the pupils there unanimously to advise teachers never to shout at pupils if they wanted pupils to learn and to flourish. And perhaps surprisingly, our findings from the two Palestinian classrooms closely mirrored findings from Meadowbank, despite the former's more explicitly authoritarian approach and its wider context of fear.

Laura Quick's (2015) research in an inner-London year 5 classroom illustrates how the children seemed to have converted their anger against a restrictive classroom regime into the playing of 'tricks'. They seemed to find these an easier way to feel confidence in their own authority than by concentrating on standard academic classroom tasks. At least through 'tricks' they could feel that they were their 'normal' (out of school) selves and thereby throw off the common feeling of being just one of the herd controlled by the teacher.

These examples suggest that although many educators believe that children learn not just by listening and absorbing passively but by engaging in inquiry and interaction, the vestiges of traditional views about learning remain in classrooms – more strongly emphasised in some than others (on the scale from the 'autocratic' to the 'consultant' teacher: Meighan and Harber, 2007). Just as assessment practice has lagged behind newer conceptions of learning and teaching (see Shepard, 2000), so has the orchestration of classrooms lagged behind these newer conceptions, partly backed up by conservative elements in society and politics and partly by 5,000 years of tradition. The result is tension for teachers, students, parents and policy-makers whose purposes for state schooling are frequently in conflict.

Children's experiences of autonomy in the classroom

The alternative to the traditional conception of learning and the traditional classroom is the understanding of learning as something that starts with the child's self. The child's self develops as the child inter-relates with people and environments. At best, in the classroom, these inter-relationships support the child to engage proactively, to self-direct and to critique the way things are, as concurrently they gain competence in a range of domain-based skills/knowledge. In other words, the alternative to the traditional conception of learning as 'being taught' by the teacher is a conception of learning (and a classroom) that places the child's autonomy at the centre. Autonomy is not a method or something that the teacher brings to the classroom: it is a deep-down understanding by a child that they have authority, that they have a valuable role to play and a contribution to make, and that they have the capacity to make changes and act on these – in the classroom and later, beyond.

Chapter 3 investigates the essential links between a child's sense of competence and both their autonomy and relatedness. All three of these are necessary for the child's well-being according to self-determination theory (Ryan and Deci, 2000). Both autonomy and relatedness are essential to achieving a sense of competence.

Achievement of attainment goals set by teachers and policy-makers has little value to children unless it is accompanied by their sense of volition and a sense of belonging within a community. These are shocking words for teachers who are pressurised to get pupils to attain prescribed targets.

In Chapter 3, I report the voices of some frustrated children who felt that they would have benefited from being allowed to use and develop their autonomy more frequently and more comprehensively in the classroom. There are examples here of young pupils proving themselves eager and able to take on responsibility for increased autonomy in the classroom. There are examples of others who developed either helpful or destructive habits to compensate for *not* feeling that they had enough autonomy.

However, where pupils have the chance to embrace autonomy, for example by choosing their own 'talk-partner' in the classroom or choosing their own processes for learning, increased proactive engagement and self-direction seem to flourish. The same is true when pupils are given a part to play by collaborating with a specially formed, balanced learning set (Collaborative Group Learning) in their classroom: not just as a one-off event but every day of their secondary school life. Here they are required to teach and to learn, to speak and to listen, to collaborate creatively and to reflect critically.

Children's autonomy was drawn upon when we asked them to participate in research projects and to express their real opinion. Some children, both in England and in Alexandria, had to learn how to do this in the moment because their classrooms had not yet prepared them in the practice of regular metalearning reflection. Other children, at Meadowbank School for example, were well used to metalearning reflection and used it to boost their own sense of autonomy in the face of fear. Both sets of children, however, appreciated and in the best cases benefited from their opportunities to express their critiques.

Children's experiences of the teacher's feedback in the classroom

One thread that runs through every classroom, whether explicitly or implicitly, is the teacher's feedback. The teacher's comments, facial expressions, behaviours and attitudes all contribute towards the child's sense of autonomy or sense of restriction, which consequently have significant influences on their learning and on how they come to conceive of themselves. In the traditional classroom, set up for teachers to transmit knowledge for pupils to reproduce, feedback was a judgement on how much information pupils had managed to retain. When learning is conceived, instead, as the construction of knowledge and the making of meaning, the traditional model of feedback no longer works. Just as the authoritarian set up of the classroom has outlived its usefulness for learning and teaching, so has the traditional model of feedback as a judgement from teacher to pupil.

In relation to how pupils described their experiences of the teacher's feedback in the classroom of Emerald Primary School and how this inspired or silenced their own voices (extended or restricted their autonomy), it is important to stress that on many occasions the teacher's feedback did indeed seem to encourage the children to act autonomously. This is likely to be the case in many classrooms. These occasions tended to be when the teacher used provocative or process-focused feedback and avoided feedback about the pupil's self. Autonomy seemed to be promoted by the teacher's feedback when her feedback encouraged pupils to show some singularity, proactivity or critical inquiry (including metasocial inquiry).

However, on other occasions, it seemed that a mismatch was evident between teachers' purposes for giving feedback and pupils' own aspirations in school. The mismatch between their own aspirations and their teachers' seemed to lead pupils to perceive the teacher's feedback as not very relevant and therefore it was not very instrumental in changing their way of seeing or being. However, the research presented here is fascinating in its portrayal of pupils clearly making connections between their social and emotional interpretations of the teacher's feedback alongside cognitive ones. Even a serious look from the teacher could make the pupils too scared and dispirited to keep trying; and at the other extreme, even a little joke or smile seemed to inspire them.

The lesson transcript excerpt provided in Chapter 4 illustrates painfully that in some classes, feedback to support individual pupils' autonomy promotion – like Vijay's – could easily get lost. Perhaps this was related to pupils' allegation that the teacher's encouragement for developing autonomy was more restricted among pupils categorised as 'low' attainers – perhaps the very people who most needed support in developing autonomy. This relates to the discussion in Chapter 5 about how those who end up in 'low ability' groups – often those from poorer backgrounds – tend to experience more spoon-feeding than autonomy-promotion. However, it is also clear that in year 5 in Emerald School, even 'high' attainers did not necessarily understand their teacher's feedback or find it useful, either for improvement of their work or for developing their autonomy. However, all groups of pupils wanted more feedback from the teacher more of the time because they wanted to be noticed and cared for as interactive human beings. They craved the teacher who was responsive and open to their needs and aspirations.

The final case study in Chapter 4 illustrates how one teacher tried to be responsive and open to his year 1 and 2 pupils by reconceptualising how the Read Write Inc. handbooks directed teachers to provide feedback to pupils. In this case, the teacher found ways to share his authority with the children themselves and listen to their voices.

Children's experiences of social class in the classroom

As Chapter 5 highlights, in many classes there are two discrete sets of pupils: middle-class and working-class. Examples in Chapter 5 illustrate how children who have more home resources, whether cultural or economic or both, manage in general to gain the teacher's attention more easily than the less-privileged children, and to carve out an authoritative sense of self for themselves in the classroom which their working-class peers find harder. The 'zombie' of social class discrimination is highlighted as still an urgent issue for schools. This is the case both from the point of view of working-class pupils having negative classroom experiences, and in particular, being negatively regarded by middle-class pupils and teachers.

Some less advantaged participants in the research by Diane Reay illustrated their sense of feeling discriminated against, being seen as less 'able' than their middle-class peers and destined to accept middle-class values obediently without negotiation. The link between so-called 'ability' grouping and social class is made clear in this chapter, illustrating how being placed in the 'bottom' set could be doubly destructive to some pupils' autonomy, thwarted both by 'low ability' and by social class. The case study of 'ability' grouping in a London primary school illustrates vividly how an atmosphere of social judgement grew up around 'ability' groups, in which the classroom emphasis on *effort* only made those in lower groups consider themselves even worse failures, because their greatest efforts did not lead to promotion to a higher group. The reason and the outcome was a class where competition dominated rather than collaboration, where children's aim was to be in the top group rather than to learn.

However, other pupils' voices warn against a 'dictatorship of no alternatives'. In Erin Gruwell's (2007) Freedom Writers' class, Alex Bloom's St George-in-the-East School, and in the classrooms of the teachers referred to across Chapters 3–4, teachers reject the traditional, authoritarian classroom in favour of one in which authority is more evenly distributed. In particular, the teachers in these classes make a practice of listening to all pupils' voices and considering them to be authoritative regardless of what the pupils can do or where they come from.

The original research projects referred to in this book

The children's words in this book are drawn from a range of classroom research projects that I have been part of recently. The names of schools, class teachers and pupils have been changed for ethical reasons. (All of these investigations were carried out in adherence to the BSA's ethical guidelines). The two main studies were:

- *2012 Emerald Primary School in Surrey, UK.* Nine year 5 pupils were observed, video-recorded and interviewed regularly over six months about their responses to the teacher's feedback (Hargreaves, 2012, 2013, 2014).
- *2013 Meadowbank Primary School just outside London, UK.* All pupils in a year 3 and a year 6 class completed a set of sentence-starters; 14 year 3 pupils and 14 year 6 pupils were interviewed; and their classes were each observed four times. The topic of research was the pupils' fear and learning (Hargreaves, 2015).

Two further studies were drawn on to a much lesser extent:

- *2013 A girls' school and a boys' school in Ramallah, Palestine.* Two year 5 classes were observed and 60 pupils were asked to complete sentence-starters about fear and learning in the classroom. Ten children were interviewed (Affouneh and Hargreaves, 2015; Hargreaves and Affouneh, 2017).
- *2015–16 Three primary schools in Alexandria, Egypt.* Eighteen lessons were observed and 394 pupils completed sentence-starters about their experiences of learning English (Hargreaves et al., 2016).

In addition to these research projects that I led myself, I am privileged also to have had access to some valuable smaller-scale research studies carried out by teachers. Several studies described in this book are drawn from classrooms whose teacher was carrying out research towards an MA degree under my supervision at UCL Institute of Education. These included the unpublished projects of the following people; whose research was conducted in or near London, UK:

- Jon Filer – who explored primary children's experiences of selecting their own talk-partners to enhance learning.
- Rob Gratton – who inquired into secondary children's experiences of collaborative group learning (CGL) in learning sets of six.
- Sean Macnamara – who researched primary children's experiences of 'ability' grouping.
- Laura Quick – who investigated primary pupils' experiences of the teacher's control and rules.
- Luke Rolls – who explored very young pupils' experiences of teacher feedback.
- Christine Yeomans – who researched secondary pupils' experiences of choice.

In addition, in order to hear many and diverse words from children, I have drawn on the more internationally-flavoured small-scale research of a few teacher-researchers who took the MA module 'Guiding Effective Learning and Teaching' under my supervision at the UCL Institute of Education during the autumn of 2015. These included Shivani Garg, Shaima Haroon, Hugh Heneghan, Konstantia Karvela, Wan Ju and Yei Je Son. I am, of course, hugely indebted to all these people who contributed so richly to this book. I am especially grateful to all the children who shared their perspectives and feelings.

1

Children's experiences of classrooms: why they matter

During a visit to a year 5 classroom in which we had asked children their views about classroom learning, Sara expressed her appreciation for being asked what she thought:

> I'm very, very joyful as this is the first time someone has come into our classroom and asked me my opinion. I am REALLY joyful! I am almost flying! I LOVE YOU! (Sara, year 5)

This book starts with children like Sara. Children like Sara are the focus of this book. The book, and the children's words within it, owe their existence to many children like Sara who have sat and talked, often in classrooms, and shared their experiences about classrooms. This book takes children's words as its essential reference point. Strange though it may seem to person-focused educators, children's words about their perspectives and feelings are notable for their *absence* in educational literature. Their insights into classrooms are rarely portrayed. This book, against the trend, provides insights into children's perspectives and feelings by presenting their own words verbatim, thereby allowing readers an opportunity to notice and reflect on these. This book is for teachers, parents and other educators who want to understand more about children's experiences in classrooms in order to improve these.

Four reasons why it is valuable to listen to children's words

Although children's views on classrooms have been rarely publicised, there are a select handful of key texts which do address these. Catherine Burke and Ian Grosvenor's (2003) survey of British pupils' perspectives on 'The school I'd like' is an excellent example. They cited one pupil who commented that, in her ideal school,

We will no longer be treated like herds of an identical animal ... It will be recognised that it is our world too. (p.7)

In other words, this student was expressing a need for pupils in classrooms to be recognised as authoritative individuals who were worthy of being listened to. Drawing on this belief, published authors have categorised at least four key reasons why it is valuable to listen to children's words about classrooms. First, children can tell us more about their own learning and what helps or hinders it than any adult can imagine and therefore, in this area, pupils are by necessity the prime authority (Burke and Grosvenor, 2003; Hopkins, 2008). Second, children *learn* through the process of talking about their own learning and its conditions (Fielding, 2004; Watkins, 2015). Third, students' engagement with classroom learning and their sense of self can be enhanced if they have had a critical voice about how learning is orchestrated and what is learnt (MacIntyre et al., 2005; Niemi et al., 2015). Fourth, children have a human right to make decisions about how and what they learn because they are valuable as human beings (UNCRC, 1989; Devine and McGillicuddy, 2016).

Children can tell us more

John Dewey, father of active and socially oriented learning approaches in the USA, warned over 100 years ago: 'Our social life has undergone a thorough and radical change. If our education is to have any meaning for life, it must pass through an equally complete *transformation*' (1899, p.14). Schooling could be said to be for the benefit of pupils, not only now but for their unknown futures. Their futures could contain more of the same schooling, including the wasteful or stressful moments described by children in Burke and Grosvenor's study. Or the future could witness a transformation of classrooms into something different. It is pupils who are in the best position to reflect on and advise on what this 'something different' might embody. They are in the strongest position actually to help adults in classrooms to reconsider the unhelpful habits that they have developed. For example, Elizabeth Hopkins (2008) explained how the pupils in her study criticised as unhelpful to their learning 'every day being the same'. The concept of 'doing what we always do' was expressed as especially negative. Given that most classrooms still do what we have always done – looking surprisingly similar to the classrooms of 5,000 years ago (Watkins, 2005) – children may be the only people who can successfully overthrow the 'dictatorship of no alternatives' in the classroom (Unger, 2011). This is especially likely given their superior expertise with digital technology. It is after all the child who articulates, in the story, that the emperor has no clothes.

Children learn through the process of talking about their own learning and its conditions

Since many educators now consider learning to be more than 'being taught' by the teacher (Watkins, 2010), they recognise that inviting pupils to express their critical views regularly allows them to construct their own knowledge and make meanings from their experiences. This is in contrast with the traditional (authoritarian) classroom which does not foster exploratory two-way interactions but instead emphasises the teacher's voice which often silences that of pupils. The picture in Figure 1.1 by a year 5 pupil is a good, standard example of the traditional classroom where the teacher talks and pupils are silent.

Michael Fielding (2004) emphasised the notion of 'student voice' on the basis of needing to deconstruct the presumptions of the present and the past. These presumptions included the tendency for adults (teachers) to talk *about* or *for* others. He contrasted this tendency with the practice of teachers and pupils speaking *with* others and pupils becoming *co-researchers* with their teachers, in classrooms. Therefore, as well as providing information to adults, when pupils talk about classrooms with their peers and teachers their learning is enhanced as well as their competence in relating with others through verbal communication. The point is that individuals actually do their learning *through* regular participation in social activities including school classroom interactions.

Figure 1.1   The traditional classroom, picture by year 5 pupil (Hargreaves et al., 2016)

Students' engagement with classroom learning and their sense of self can be enhanced if they have had a critical voice about how learning happens and what is learnt

Several published studies have noted that pupils' talk can not only lead to pupils' increased engagement in learning but also to an enhanced sense of self if children have a chance critically to evaluate their learning situation. In the research of Donald MacIntyre and colleagues (2005), the pupils themselves told the researchers that, for richer learning, they needed more opportunities in the classroom for fostering a sense of agency and ownership. John Dewey (1899, p.14) used the word 'self-direction' in this context. He stressed the urgency for individual pupils to communicate and then to act, rather than just to listen:

> The ordinary schoolroom, with its rows of ugly desks placed in geometrical order, crowded together ... it is all made 'for listening' ... The attitude of listening means, comparatively speaking, passivity and absorption ... the moment children act they individualise themselves; they cease to be a mass, and become the intensely distinctive beings that we are acquainted with out of school. (p.15)

Educator Alfie Kohn (1996) has written about potential ways of increasing the distribution of authority among teachers and pupils in classrooms so that pupils have more opportunities to act on their own decisions:

> Each aspect of life in a classroom offers an invitation to think about what decisions might be turned over to students or negotiated with students individually and collectively. (p.85)

Paulo Freire (1972), famously critical educator from Brazil, described how the 'oppressor' (authoritarian teacher) was characterised by the tendency to *prescribe to* rather than *negotiate with* the 'oppressed' (pupil):

> Thus, the behaviour of the oppressed is a prescribed behaviour, following as it does the guidelines of the oppressor ... Freedom would require them to eject this image and replace it with autonomy and responsibility. (pp.23–4)

These words reflected Plato's 2000-year-old description of a slave. Dewey (2011) portrayed this as someone who, like the school student in some classrooms, 'accepts from another the purposes which control his [or her] conduct ... whose service they do not understand and have no personal interest in' (pp.48–49). Freire believed that any situation in which some people prevented others from engaging in active inquiry was 'one of violence' and oppression (1972, p.58). By preventing active inquiry in classrooms, including the chance to express and explore views critically or to make decisions and act upon them, students were denied the opportunities for growing up into mature, autonomous people who could start critically reflecting on their world in order to make the world a better place. This mattered at two levels:

- at the individual level, human beings could not enjoy full humanity without exercising their autonomy; and
- at the social level, society could not remain peaceable if large sections of it were kept silent by the rest.

Children have a human right to make decisions about how and what they learn because they are valuable as human beings

Clive Harber (2015) suggested that in a world context, most classrooms

> reproduce and perpetrate – not only the socio-economic and political inequalities of the surrounding society, including gender relationships, but also the violent relationships that often go with them. (p.243)

Classrooms can either be places where traditional and often oppressive power relationships are sustained, or they can act as models of transformed social and political relationships, where every child learns to understand their own and others' rights, including the right to talk and to participate in decisions that affect them. By asking pupils to talk about their experiences in classrooms and to describe these in relation to their own aspirations, identity and personality, the inequalities within the classroom and beyond may become a clearer focus of attention (and see Chapter 5 on social class inequality in the classroom). Dympna Devine and Deirdre McGillicuddy (2016) have suggested that despite the neo-liberal thrust of education today, there is concurrently a global recognition of the need to value children for themselves, including championing children's rights to express critiques about classrooms. They suggested:

> The UNCRC [United Nations Convention on the Rights of the Child, 1989] has been pivotal in this changing discourse, providing a template for working towards, albeit minimum, standards of rights for all children, including provisions directly related to education ... Article 29 defines the

purpose of education. This latter embraces holistic concepts that include recognition [during education] of culture, identity, and the development of the child's personality in a spirit of peace, tolerance and equality. Of equal importance are more general principles expressed in Articles 2, 3 and 12 that underpin all other articles. These relate to non-discrimination with respect to different groups of children (birth, race, colour, sex, language, religion, politics, birth or other status), *as well as the right for children to have a say in matters directly affecting them* ... This can be articulated not only in terms of considering the quality *of* teaching and learning that children receive, but also in/equalities *in* learning that may be provided to different groups of children. (pp.424–5; my emphases)

In other words, these authors suggested that a transformation towards increased recognition of children's rights in classrooms was gradually occurring, especially in relation to how children actually experienced the quality of classroom learning and to their having some control over this. This book aims to feed into this transformation.

Pupils' perceptions are different from adults'

Recently I noticed my daughter, Jasmine, doing her GCSE revision at the living-room table while sending WhatsApp messages on her phone and watching YouTube videos on her laptop. I remembered that for my own studies, I literally studied in the silence of a cold attic, unconnected with the rest of the world, with the attic door carefully closed. When I mentioned to her how I used to study and why it was effective, her response, quite reasonably, was:

❝ Well, I'm not like you.   ❞

One good reason to explore children's perspectives of and feelings about classrooms is this disparity, noted by Piaget (1925), between how teachers conceive of classrooms and how pupils do. Piaget suggested that the starting point for teachers' effective planning was to acknowledge these differences between children's and adults' ways of seeing (and feeling) the classroom. The mistake of traditional classrooms was the expectation that the child's experience of the world would be, or should be, similar to that of an adult. Noddings (2005) illustrated this same point with descriptions of the gaps and misunderstandings between children's expressed needs and the adult's inferred ones in the classroom. As a result of these gaps and misunderstandings, the classroom became an embodiment of assumptions and interpretations by adults rather than a place which started with how children saw and felt the classroom.

This disparity is important because, as explored further in Chapter 2, the teacher's authority (the right/power to make decisions and have them acted on) can only be legitimately sustained if the teacher has her/his pupils' willing consent to obey. This is only likely to happen if the teacher understands or at least values and respects the experiences of the pupils, and also makes efforts to share rather than protect her/his decision-making powers. If this is not the case, the teacher's *authority* may slip into *authoritarianism* – in which teacher coercion replaces pupil consent. A classroom based on coercion rather than consent is likely to reduce children's opportunities for proactive engagement and self-direction, which has potential long-term disadvantages for the pupils as well as the society they will become part of as adults.

In a significant piece of research by Alex Moore (2013), the disparity between teachers' and pupils' perceptions and feelings became vividly evident. In a nutshell, while the teacher seemed to focus primarily on pupils' cognitive gains, the pupils were much more motivated by affective and social factors: specifically, how they felt, and their relationship with the teacher and each other. In Moore's words:

> Whereas the teachers self-perceived as caring, loving practitioners who had their students' best interests at heart, the children's view of their teachers tended to be of a group of adults who did not understand their differences or their needs, who did not care for or about them, and who did little to make learning the enjoyable experience it was supposed to be. (p.285)

In this situation, the pupils were therefore carrying out actions in the classroom like the slave described above, accepting from another the purposes which control conduct, 'whose service they do not understand and have no personal interest in' (Dewey, 2011). Without the teacher's understanding or personal interest in the pupils' own agenda, it is unlikely that children will engage proactively or responsibly with the learning s/he offers them.

Another example of the mismatch described by Piaget – probably common in many traditional classrooms – became clear during our recent project carried out in Alexandria, Egypt. A startling mismatch was detected between the pupils' stated purposes for learning English and the way English was actually taught to them in the classroom (Hargreaves et al., 2016). In this study, nearly half of the 394 ten-year-old children in the study said that their aim for learning English was to *speak English with others*, and over a quarter of them saw the purpose of learning English as for use when *travelling abroad*. And yet in the nine 45-minute English classes we observed, there were almost no occasions on which the pupils practised speaking English at all. Despite the pressure on these pupils to do well in their exams, it seemed likely that they would take a more genuine interest in engaging with the English lesson in the future if it addressed directly their deeply-held personal goals. Instead, those who had access, practised speaking English using YouTube clips and talking with older siblings at home.

A very different kind of study noted that teachers and pupils differed in their experiences of which events actually *happened* in the classroom. In a national survey carried out by the Ministry of Education in Macedonia (2016, p.38), the following results were found: pupils estimated that about 32 per cent of class time was taken up with group activities, while teachers rated it as 63 per cent (nearly double!); pupils estimated that 24 per cent of time was taken up discussing topics chosen by the students while teachers rated this as 57 per cent of the time (more than double); pupils thought that about 25 per cent of time was spent in carrying out their own research activities while teachers rated this at 53 per cent of the time (more than double). This study simply reinforced the different perceptions of pupils and teachers and emphasised the need for talk among both groups in order to understand what is happening within the classroom from both groups' perspectives, and which activities might be most helpful to achieve each group's aspirations.

Children's classroom learning: a cognitive, affective, social and physical experience?

What is meant by learning and experience

Borrowing from Marton and Booth's (1997) construct of phenomenography, I propose that 'learning' and 'experience' are more closely linked than traditional models of learning implied. *Learning* and *experience* can both be conceptualised as multi-faceted, involving the child's cognition (knowing, thinking, understanding), affect (feelings, emotions), motivation (incentives, personal goals, aspirations) and their understanding of the context (both immediate and wider). To *experience* the classroom implies being affected or influenced by the cognitive, affective, motivational and contextual aspects of *being in* the classroom. These diverse experiences become *learning* when the child tries to make sense of these or attributes some meaning to them.

I stress experiences as the basis for learning in order to illustrate the thinness of how the word 'learning' has traditionally (and popularly) been used: its traditional use has tended to ignore the affective, social and physical aspects of the child that are, none the less, always dominant in the classroom. It has also neglected the fact that children make meaning, construct knowledge – or *learn* – by drawing on all of these aspects. Many educators and parents still focus on learning as cognitive 'input' and attaining learning 'objectives'. But the cognitive aspects of the child are only one part of her/his meaning-making, knowledge-constructing tool-kit. The exclusively cognitive view of learning is a relic from the traditional classroom in which the transmission of information was emphasised (see Chapter 2). Learning, instead, can more comprehensively be said to refer to the child's past experiences, including relationships, *and the meaning/knowledge they have constructed from these*; their current experiences and relationships *and the meaning/knowledge they are currently creating from these*; and the *ways in which they will respond* cognitively, affectively, socially and physically to future experiences and relationships, based on what has come beforehand. All these aspects will be functioning in the classroom and the full spectrum of these aspects constitute the basis of children's learning there.

Pupils' learning through relationship

Anne Edwards (2005) suggested that it was through the *relational experience* that the child came both to conceive of and to act on the world in a particular way. In other words, individuals learn and develop through participation in social activities in the world. Tone Saevi described the teacher's role with the child in the classroom as something ongoing, non-tangible and fluid, as a 'relational and existential endeavour without a specified end'. She believed that: 'As an adult I ought to ask myself what [students] learn from *being with* me' (2015, p.347; my emphases). Saevi continued:

> The pedagogical relationship is vital to children to allow them to speak of that which can only partly be spoken of ... What is lived and experienced is more basic and must have existential priority over what is thought and said. (p.349)

However, as a teacher, it is possible to hold two parallel conceptions of learning simultaneously and act as if both are appropriate. In fact, many of us find ourselves trying to do just that. There is one voice saying that learning means acquiring cognitive content and reaching academic targets: schools emphasise this version because of policy pressure relating to global economic competition. Another voice inside the head of many teachers says that learning means having a nurturing relationship with the child: we became teachers because we wanted to support and inspire young people; as teachers, we therefore want to nurture all aspects of the child into appropriate ways of being and seeing, through the relationship we have with the child. However, while we are pressured by policy to focus on cognitive and measurable outcomes, this focus often comes at the expense of affective and social (relational) aspects. In the chapters in this book, especially in Chapter 2, I explore how this pressure sometimes leads teachers unwittingly to buy into authoritarian approaches to classrooms in which the cognitive aspects of the child are directed, rather than the relational aspects being nurtured.

Alex Moore's (2013) research suggested that pupils' classroom experiences could be heavily influenced by any of the following relational aspects of the classroom, all of which would be likely to dominate the child's capacity to process cognitive input:

- emotional states brought about by factors 'external' to the immediate teacher–student relationship (e.g. friendship or family issues);
- the teacher's response to these;
- the teacher's own emotional behaviour (e.g. displays of anger or stress);
- the way in which the teacher (as well as the other students) displays affection and (in a pupil's words) 'love' to the student, demonstrable both through words and through a reward system.

The child's relationship to the teacher as an *authority* is likely to affect significantly the child's experience of the classroom, and thereby their learning (see Chapter 2). Saevi suggested that in the classroom, the experience of pupil and teacher *being together* constitutes, and at the same time brings about, learning and guides the child to *see themselves in a different way*. How the adult behaves, and how the adult relates specifically to the child, gradually brings about cognitive, affective or social change in the child as they make sense of this relating. They gradually come to see themselves in a different way – at best, in a positive different way.

Based on his research work with adults, Jack Mesirow (2006) suggested that 'transformative learning' involved seeing oneself in a positive different way. This entailed understanding more fully one's role in the world in relation to others and in relation to social structures. According to Tone Saevi (2015), children learn most transformationally in this positive sense through the experience of being with teachers who are responsive to their individual existence and open to their dynamic and unpredictable development. Saevi stressed that the pedagogic relationship had to do with 'the necessary tension between authority and freedom expressed in the asymmetric relationship between adult and child' (p.345). When this tension is dealt with by the teacher in a responsive and open way, the child's transformation is likely to consist of seeing themselves and their role more positively. However, if the teacher is neither *responsive* to the child's individual existence nor *open* to their dynamic and unpredictable development, this does not signify that the child will not change. When the child's relationship to authority is not sensitively managed in the classroom, *the child may come to see her/himself in a different way, but this time in a more negative way, as less powerful, less competent or less valued than they previously believed.*

The meanings children derive from their classroom relationships may not be observed by an outsider or even perceived by the child (Torrance, 2012); but in the sense of *seeing oneself in a different way*, learning may be happening little by little as the child engages (or fails to engage) with others in the classroom, especially the teacher. Once a student makes sense in a particular way in the classroom, this then can become the basis for future action, which in turn can reinforce the stance taken, forming either a positive or negative loop (Williams and Ivey, 2001). This book explores children's experiences of relating to the teacher and the opportunities this entails for changing how they see themselves as a person.

The child's encounter with the teacher will evidently be a crucial factor in her/his learning. However, encounters will also take place with other children. In this sense, learning can come about through *building knowledge as part of doing things with others* (Watkins, 2005, p.14). Others may be peers in class, children in the same so-called 'ability' group, children in a previous classroom or brothers and sisters at home. The important point is that, whether it is recognised explicitly or not, all learning occurs within the context of relational experiences. It is with this relationship-based aspect of children's learning in mind that I consider children's experiences in classrooms in this book.

A focus on the classroom emphasises each pupil's experience

The recent film called 'The Class' (*Entre Les Murs* in French but renamed 'The Class') was distinctive because it actually portrayed how things happened between the walls of a normal classroom in France. The tradition of the teacher shutting the classroom door carefully behind them and savouring the privacy of her/his own classroom, as depicted in this film, still runs deep in England's schooling system too. But what really happens between those walls each day and how does each pupil experience it?

When my son, Wesley, arrives home from school each day and I ask him 'How was your day?' it's rare to receive more than a one word answer: 'Okay'. But what this word really denotes, I have no way of knowing. He possibly feels that it would be too complex to tell me what it was really like. Since the safeguarding of children became an increased priority in schools in England, access to classrooms has become more difficult for other adults, so even less is known about what happens there. But it is here that pupils have many formative – both positive and negative – experiences, uncharted even by the pupils themselves and shut carefully away from the outside world like the attic. Schools have prospectuses and documents laying out how things should be done. But the classroom is not the school. Every classroom is different. And every pupil's experience of every classroom is different.

In one primary school where I planned to interview pupils, a few parents were worried about me talking to their children and observing classes. They refused to sign the consent form. They said that they did not know how their children would be 'used'. What struck me as strange was the fact that the children's teacher and teaching assistant worked with their children all day every day without the parents knowing what happened to them from one week to the next. Perhaps these parents perceived that the classroom adults had a legitimate authority that I did not have as a researcher.

All those hours, days and years that children sit in classrooms: What's it really like for them? How will it affect them now and in later life? And is this really the richest experience we can offer them?

My purpose in this book is to explore these issues from the perspective of the pupils themselves. The book asks the question of how children talk about their experiences of authority or authoritarianism in the classroom, and how they perceive that their relationship with the teacher influences them and their learning (Chapter 2); whether they experience and exercise autonomy in the classroom and whether/how this might happen more extensively (Chapter 3); it explores children's descriptions of how they experience the teacher's feedback in the classroom and how this might influence or silence their own voices (Chapter 4); it explores how social class might be perpetuated in the classroom and what children's own experiences are of this (Chapter 5).

Schiro's purposes for schooling: the effective classroom is one that achieves its purpose

Whether children's experiences in classrooms are in fact the richest we can offer them, and how the 'richest' is defined, depends on each person's values and what they believe the purpose of schooling to be. This in turn will influence what they believe 'learning' to involve. When authors talk about 'effective' classrooms, it is sometimes assumed that this means that the classroom 'gets' good test results. However, whether a classroom is effective or not depends what the end-point is against which it is evaluated. Good test results alone are not the only possible outcomes of a classroom.

Michael Schiro (2013) has categorised four ideologies or philosophies of state-funded schooling which help define the effective classroom in terms of how well four different purposes are achieved (cited in Moore, 2015, p.150). These purposes are referred to throughout the chapters that follow in this book as a framework for considering the conflicting contexts within which classrooms are situated and how effectively they are seen to be operating according to each purpose.

1. 'Scholar academics' believe that *'the purpose of education is to help children learn the accumulated knowledge of our culture: that of the academic disciplines.'* Valuable topics are divided into subject areas, for which knowledge and facts are identified as most important for pupils to learn at particular stages of their schooling. This purpose fits with that of traditional classrooms where the emphasis is on the transmission from teachers to students of the 'accumulated knowledge' of their culture. Those teachers who hold this ideology would therefore value those conditions in classrooms that best foster memorisation, retention and understanding such as focusing on pupils' physical and emotional comfort, quietness for memorising and peaceful peer–peer and teacher–pupil relationships to ensure minimal emotional or physical distraction from cognitive action. This is what Bernstein referred to as the *collectionist* approach (1971, p.47). In this book, children's experiences of classrooms dominated by this approach are explored.

2. Advocates, on the other hand, of the 'social efficiency ideology' 'believe that the purpose of schooling is to efficiently meet the needs of society by training youth to function as future mature contributing members of society'. For supporters of this ideology, classroom learning is about learning skills and knowledge which will be useful for future employment, such as employability, flexibility, collaborative skills plus practical expertise. In such classrooms, the relevance pupils see in their curriculum to their real future (economic) lives will be of key importance, as well as pupils' practical experiences in particular expert areas. In my experience, this is the purpose often assumed by pupils: that school is there to prepare them for employment in the society that already exists.

3. In the 'learner centred' ideology, 'the goal of education is the growth of individuals: his or her own unique intellectual, social, emotional and physical attributes.' In classrooms which entertain the learner-centred ideology, the pupil's everyday cognitive, affective, social and physical development and flourishing will be the principal means and ends of classroom learning, including how pupils perceive themselves, how they relate to each other, and how they relate to other adults. This approach relates to Bernstein's *integrationist*

approach (1971, p.47). Many of the children's words in this book relate to children's affective, social and physical experiences of classrooms.

4. The 'social reconstruction ideology' suggests that the purpose of education is the development of a 'critically educated citizenry able to engage reflectively and reflexively with the wider society, opening up greater possibilities for radical societal change'. In classrooms where this philosophy is highly valued, it will not just be the individual's development and flourishing that matters but also their relationships with the fluctuating social contexts outside the classroom and pupils' awareness of justice and power imbalances both within and beyond the classroom. The nurturing of pupils' critical reflection and their awareness of the historical, sociological and political contexts of schooling will be essential components of their day-to-day classroom experiences as illustrated in particular in Chapter 5 of this book.

2

Authority and authoritarianism in the classroom

> ❛ Everything just goes blank [when I'm writing] ... Sometimes I feel like everyone's like so much taller than me ... and then the teacher's like really, really big. (Sapphire, year 6) ❜

Figure 2.1   'The teacher's like, really, really big!' Picture by year 5 pupil (Hargreaves et al., 2016)

In this chapter, children's experiences of the teacher's authority, sometimes manifested as authoritarianism, is explored. In particular, the chapter investigates the influences that an authoritarian approach can have on the day-to-day organisation and culture in the classroom. It aims to lay bare, in some detail, the negative aspects of children's experiences in the many authoritarian classrooms the world over. My experience of working with other teachers is that they do not always realise that they are situated within an authoritarian school framework, nor how much children can suffer as a result of this. This chapter aims to raise awareness of both of these. As Gale Macleod and colleagues suggested (2012), this is important because:

> Understanding the child–teacher authority relationship is central to understanding what goes on in classrooms. (p.494)

This chapter also provides some theoretical explanations for the persistence of authoritarian approaches across the world, in countries with democratic and autocratic governments alike. It aims to draw attention to children's recommendation that classrooms depend to a greater extent on children's own authority rather than relying on the teacher's authoritarianism.

This chapter draws particularly on research carried out in two sets of London classrooms in two different primary schools. In the first, Meadowbank Primary School, pupils talked about the fear they felt during their learning, often due to the authoritarian context within which they operated, despite the teachers' best attempts to support their self-directed learning. In the second, pupils described to researcher Laura Quick the 'tricks' they used to overcome the teacher's perceived authoritarianism and to overcome their anger that resulted from the teacher's rules and control. Paulo Freire's (1972, 1998) work is drawn on substantially in this chapter because of his classic role in theorising this topic along with Clive Harber's (2015) writing on authoritarianism in schools internationally.

The teacher's 'authority' is the teacher's legitimate right or power, based on her/his expertise, to orchestrate the classroom in which pupils recognise the value of her/his expertise. On the other hand, the word 'authoritarian', in the context of the classroom, suggests that the teacher asserts her/his authority using coercion rather than consent. In other words, children obey her/him because s/he threatens them with fearsome consequences if they do not do what s/he tells them: the children are not obeying because they believe in the value of her/his rules and orders but because they are afraid. This tends to be the situation in many classrooms in the world today and is likely to be upheld so long as the teacher's control rather than the pupils' authority is emphasised. It is essential to remember, however, that there are already many teachers and pupils who are striving towards classrooms within which authority is better distributed among teacher and pupils. Some of the alternative ways they use to orchestrate classrooms are explored in the rest of the book.

The potentially restrictive influence of authoritarianism in classrooms around the world

Carl Rogers (1957) described 'unconditional positive regard' as essential to the establishment of a free and equal relationship between two people, including between pupil and teacher. He explained:

> It means that there are no *conditions* of acceptance, no feeling of 'I like you only if you are thus and so'. It means a 'prizing' of the person ...'. (p.5)

In terms of the classroom, 'unconditional positive regard' means that the teacher acknowledges, respects and draws on every child's authority, using her/his own authority to guide them. S/he does not distribute care and attention only to those who obey, who think like s/he does or who attain high marks.

Authority can be seen as having a right or having the power to make decisions and get them acted on. In a classroom of distributed authority, the teacher recognises this right and encourages this power within each pupil. On the other hand, the teacher–pupil relationship in an authoritarian system is a 'dependence relationship in which one person is dominant and another or others dependent' (Meighan and Harber, 2007, p.238), in stark contrast to the relationship suggested by Rogers. While dependence does not necessarily imply domination by the non-dependent partner, in classrooms this seems to be how it is played out or how children experience it. Children's dependence on the *teacher as knowledge-giver* seems traditionally to have sanctioned teachers to dominate pupils, rather than to caution teachers to take extra care. This unequal and potentially destructive relationship between teacher and pupil is likely to be taken for granted by many pupils, parents and teachers the world over, even today. Currently the authoritarian classroom is the norm and probably has been since the earliest known classrooms of 3000 BC (Watkins, 2005) which, even 5,000 years ago, were laid out so as to allow the teacher to control a set of dependent students.

Some authoritarian tendencies have been attributed to the church. Although the influences of the Christian religion in Britain may be less obvious today than previously, their legacy remains discretely embedded:

> The Christian doctrine of the Fall, that [humans are] born in sin and can reach a state of beatitude only through serving God and with the aid of divine grace, has deeply influenced education throughout the West. The idea seems to be firmly embedded in Western consciousness ... Because of it, education has been regarded as a moral discipline: *the child is naturally evil and can be saved only with the aid of strict control, denial, and authority.* His [or her] natural propensities will lead him [or her] astray and should, therefore, not be indulged. (Nash, 1966, p.103; my emphasis)

In some parts of the world, this belief is still openly held and the biblical text from Proverbs 13, verse 24 is used to legitimise the use of corporal punishment: *Whoever spares the rod hates their children, but the one who loves their children is careful to discipline them.*

In contrast with John Dewey's (1899) emphasis on the need for the bustle of creative activity in the classroom in order for meaningful learning to flourish, pupils from authoritarian classrooms around the world have reported some fearsomely restrictive experiences. For these pupils, experiences can be tough, even in classrooms where teachers are trying to promote children's autonomy and to make classrooms enjoyable places. However, it has also become clear from these studies that different children feel oppressed by a variety of different aspects of authoritarian classrooms and that, perhaps as a result of this, some children are thriving more than others, but many are feeling disempowered and some are feeling distressed. This is where Freire's words seem relevant, that as a teacher it is not enough simply to accept the authoritarian schooling system that we are so accustomed to. The fact that I may not be a policy-maker or (in Freire's words) a therapist, 'Does not excuse me for ignoring the suffering or the disquiet that one of my students may be going through' (1998, p.128).

Erica Southgate (2003) has reported on the classroom memories of many students she interviewed from Australia. She theorised that the teacher's ultimate power *over* rather than *with* students led to conditions 'where fear and shame blossom, and that this immobilises students, with often lasting effects' (p.91). She described how punishments, dependent on the teacher's seemingly unfettered power, deliberately promoted feelings of *isolation* among students and she related how this feeling of isolation could have a lasting emotional impact on one's sense of self. In particular, her interviewees described students' lasting memories of the teacher's voice in the classroom: how kind words were long remembered but how the teacher's shouting voice could be so terrifying that it led to feelings of helplessness and passivity and the desire to shrink in size to hide away (see the tiny pupils in the picture at the start of this chapter, for example!). Southgate's informants often used military metaphors to describe the teachers' actions, such as having questions 'fired at' them. And she noted:

> Students in these stories do not move when the teacher yells, nor do they communicate with each other, except in a kind of shared bodily language of fear. (p.94)

Punishments in which the 'punished' child was made conspicuous – in isolation – supported Michel Foucault's claim that 'visibility is a trap, a trap that not only immobilises, but also wounds' (1978, p.200, cited in Southgate, 2003, p.100).

Dympna Devine, researching in two Irish primary schools around the same time as Southgate (2003), noted the restrictions that (authoritarian) classrooms imposed on young pupils' freedom of *physical* movement, whereby children would be physically positioned to pay maximum attention to the teacher's talk. She cited one child as saying that it seemed as though:

> The teacher is in the middle of the room with a great big remote control and you have to do everything she says or you will get into trouble. (p.68)

The physical positioning of these primary aged children was also controlled in that they were expected to sit up straight, look neat and tidy, try hard all the time and not become too comfortable: supposedly as signs of respect for the teacher's author-ity. Devine pointed, however, to some teachers' 'tendency to utilise discipline for the purposes of containment and social control rather than necessarily for learning and self empowerment' (p.65). The pupils noted, for example, that the teachers used girls as the physical means for stopping boys being distracted, by creating boy-girl-boy-girl seating arrangements in the classroom – in which the children had no say. Girls' physical comfort, well-being and learning generally were in this case sacri-ficed to teachers' perception that girls should be the bearers of internalised adult norms. Unlike the slightly older children, the younger children generally accepted the teacher's all-powerful role of law-giver and protector, but when teachers' rules were randomly changed or when the teacher refused to sort out individual feuds, then even the younger children felt betrayed.

As Carolyn Jackson found in her (2010) research, because teachers depended on authoritarian structures in order to control both pupils' behaviour and to receive institutional approval themselves, teachers often resorted to threats of fearsome punishment when classroom practices were challenged. Even teachers who clearly cared very much about their pupils' well-being most of the time, at other times threatened them with punishments. This was often because of the punishments they themselves feared if student exam results did not meet school targets. This coercion felt – and then exerted – by the teacher is illustrated in the following example from a school in Pakistan. In her MA research, head teacher Saima Haroon described how 'When I spoke to Miss Janin [teacher] about the contrast between her pleas-ant and chirpy behaviour with me and the coercive strategies being adopted in [the teacher's] class, she answered:

Teacher Janin: You and I are colleagues. When you saw me in the morning in my classroom, I was performing the role of a teacher. There are specific things I need to do and ways I need to act with my students if I want to achieve the desired result.

SH: Does being harsh with the students ever bother you?

Teacher Janin: When I'm in the teacher role, my job is to make sure that the students learn as much as possible. To do that, I need to create an envi-ronment where fear acts as a motivator. They perform better because they are afraid of me and then there is fear of failure.

In other words, teachers' fear of not fulfilling their own role as required may lead them to coerce their students through threat of punishment, even when they are genuinely caring people (and in Teacher Janin's mind, perhaps *because* she is a genuinely caring person).

The assumption underlying harsh punishments on children may originally have been that, among the masses of children in the state school system, children needed to be coerced to learn: and that lack of learning was due to laziness rather than due to what was taught and how it was taught. If learning meant sitting listening to the teacher and absorbing information, then pupils needed to be coerced to sit and listen and absorb. Ironically, a study by Marie-Christine Opdenakker and Jan Van Damme (2000) concluded that this assumption about working-class students (the 'masses') may have been counter-intuitive: these researchers found that many disengaged and disaffected working-class pupils' achievement and well-being were negatively affected by a coercive, disciplinarian approach. In terms of learning (rather than teaching), all pupils are likely to be disadvantaged by teaching in which learning is defined as being made to sit, listen and absorb: however, Opdenakker and Van Damme's work pointed to particularly negative effects for working-class pupils when they were coerced into doing so using harsh or militaristic means.

Children's words: how the dominant teacher's stress or anger could be experienced by children in the classroom

The teacher's dominant role in the classroom stemmed from the traditional belief that the teacher had the 'authority' to control learners' minds and bodies because of her/his unrivalled role as knowledge-giver. This authority seems to have given some teachers the sense of *not* being subject to common rules of human politeness in the classroom with students. In particular, they felt permitted to express their anger to pupils when pupils were not doing what the teacher wanted. Alex Moore's (2013) research illustrated that pupils' classroom experiences could be heavily influenced by the teacher's own emotional behaviour (e.g. displays of anger or stress) because of her dominant role and the lack of clear limits to her rules. Moore suggested that when children's needs were unmet or unexpressed because of their fear about the teacher's angry response, this could reduce the child's capacity and willingness to learn at all; or it could impel children into shallow or pseudo learning activities in which the principal object was to win immediate, short-term teacher approval rather than to learn in order to increase their competence. These findings were also reflected in a range of classrooms beyond Moore's research to which I have had access. In these situations too, the teacher's privileged position as the sole authority in the classroom could allow her to express anger freely, leading to an unwelcome sense of powerlessness and anxiety on the part of pupils which subsequently inhibited their learning. For example, teacher-researcher and MA-student Hugh Heneghan reported the words of his primary pupils in London, UK, that when they were under stress or pressure, teachers became more angry and less nurturing. Pupil Sarah told him:

> Sometimes [the teacher] can be stressed. If the class has not done well [in the tests] she can be stressed or angry because the class has let her down.

Her friend added:

> Teachers are tired and stressed out but want to make children's lives better ... they stress and shout at those children who don't pay attention because they [the children] go to bed too late.

Behind these comments, one can imagine Sarah and her friend's teacher struggling to get all her pupils up to the levels prescribed by school, the teacher herself being subject to the seemingly unfettered and sometimes misdirected power of government interventions.

Yei Je Son, a teacher-researcher carrying out MA research in schools in South Korea, found a similar fear of the teacher's anger among pupils there. Their experiences emphasised the difference between ordinary relationships and the relationship between teacher and pupils. A 12-year-old pupil, Euenji, articulated the prolonged effects of such displays of anger by the teacher, which muted her learning:

> When I had a fight with my friends, either I or my friends tried to make up within an hour. But when the teacher was angry with the class, I couldn't do anything. Even though I was not being told off, I kept studying her face and couldn't concentrate on learning. She didn't notice my feeling.

Euenji attributed the stark impact of the teacher's anger to the fact that students were extremely dependent on the teacher for their smooth passage through school.

The following words from three children in a primary school in Greece illustrated a similarly distressing experience of schooling for pupils due to a teacher's display of stress (drawn from the work of Konstantia Karvela, teacher-researcher and MA-student):

> **Dimitra:** I usually feel bad when Ms Anna [teacher] seems angry or upset. I start thinking that she might start scolding us.
>
> **Elena:** I don't like it when Ms Anna doesn't let me finish what I want to say or doesn't pay attention to me ... That makes me think that she doesn't care because [she believes] what I have to say isn't important ... and that really hurts my feelings ...
>
> **KK:** Why do you think she doesn't let you finish?
>
> **Elena:** Sometimes she is in a hurry and she doesn't listen to me at all! and if Ms Anna doesn't care, no one really cares ...
>
> **Katerina:** Sometimes I get so upset that I want to cry ... but I can't do that because they will say that I am a baby and stuff.

There is a similarity here with research done in India whereby one teenage student reflected:

> ❧ It was annoying to see that the teachers could freely express their emotions in class, but we were expected to exercise emotional control. (Miheer in MA student teacher-researcher Shivani Garg's research) ❧

These examples illustrated how the teacher's role as the authority in the classroom could morph into an authoritarian approach to classroom management whereby they found themselves (often unwittingly) coercing children to do things by playing on their emotional vulnerability. This became possible because of children's dependence on the teacher and because the teacher's emotional outbursts tended to be unmonitored.

In this way, children sit in the classroom with the angry or over-stretched teacher, powerless to challenge the teacher's outbursts; but also unlikely to learn meaningfully. If this is the model that pupils learn to accept during all their school years, then this is the model they are likely to support in adult life: the model of domination by some, submission by the rest; directives from some, silence among the rest (Pace and Hemmings, 2006). In other words, authoritarianism in the classroom can sow the seeds of social divisions in adult society (see Chapter 5).

The structures of authoritarian classrooms

Adam Lefstein (2002, p.1631–2 based on Foucault, 1978) summarised four systemic surveillance structures which have been embodied in the authoritarian pedagogic approach and enabled pupils' actions to be tightly controlled in classrooms:

1. *Distribution of pupils in particular, prescribed groupings, often to ensure pupils do not communicate with each other.* For example, pupils sit at desks that are spaced apart or which prevent pupils' eye contact with each other.
2. *Teachers' control of the activity, whereby the teacher dictates the content, pace and order of pupils' activities.* This dictation might take a more autocratic form or a more democratic one.
3. *Hierarchical observation, whereby figures and structures more powerful than the teacher are ever-present to enforce obedience.* In schools today, figures representing these might be the deputy head or principal, local officials or even government inspectors. These figures keep teachers in control and keep other controlling structures in place whose influence cascades down to pupils.
4. *The normalising judgement or examination, by which pupils are labelled as failing or otherwise.* Current examples of how this judgement is conveyed include standardised tests or exams as well as 'ability' grouping.

Foucault (1978) accounted for the development of these authoritarian pedagogic structures by describing how the major problem facing 18th-century social organisers, including organisers of schools, was how to manage multitudes of people in relatively limited spaces so that productive outcomes were maximised and threats to the organisers' control minimised (Lefstein, 2002, p.1629). Educational outcomes were seen as similar to factory outcomes: pupils were seen as recipients of information from the teacher which they should be able later to reproduce. Against this background, authoritarian schooling, based on the idea of learning as absorbing and reproducing knowledge, developed in most western countries. This western model has also been exported worldwide through colonialism. Minimal focus has therefore been placed on children's aspirations, perceptions and feelings during the process.

Authoritarian institutions traditionally draw on the ideology outlined by Michael Schiro as of 'Scholar Academics', who hold that 'the purpose of education is to help children learn the accumulated knowledge of our culture: that of the academic disciplines' (2013, p.4). This ideology supports the status quo in society, supporting those in power to remain powerful, sometimes even by coercive means. The emphasis here is therefore on transmitting the 'accumulated knowledge' from authoritative teacher to unauthoritative student whose job is to absorb and reproduce without comment.

As illustrated in Chapter 3 which follows, many challenges can be put to this model. But how classrooms are judged depends how learning is defined. Once the idea is challenged, of children as factory workers who hold no authority and whose job is to reproduce information, then learning takes on a very different perspective. If learning is seen as the construction of meaningful knowledge by an authoritative but inexperienced pupil, then the classroom needs to be orchestrated in quite a different way. Learning is thereby seen to be about making meaning and building relationships among ideas and among people. To improve learning outcomes under this model, it is therefore essential to provide for the learners' affective, social and physical needs as well as their cognitive ones. Learning in this definition is an affective, social and physical pursuit as well as a cognitive one. Many teachers in thousands of classrooms attempt in this way to encourage learning as knowledge-construction and meaning-making – individual or collaborative. But the association between learning and authoritarian classrooms is still hard to shift, particularly because it is linked to the elite in society sustaining power (as discussed by Freire, see below).

Children's words: the link between the authoritarian classroom and children's fear

It is only when learning is seen as different from 'being taught' (Watkins, 2010) that the problem with coercion in the classroom becomes really clear. If learning means a pupil constructing knowledge, making meanings, making relationships, then learners are drawing on affective, social, physical and cognitive aspects of their experiences in order to learn. Teachers need to nurture and help them develop their affective, social, physical and cognitive capacities in order to learn most richly. Coercion, often leading to fear, is likely to inhibit or damage the child's development of these. While discipline is necessary to maintain appropriate behaviour, this must not be confused with the conditions that support appropriate learning. John Holt linked coercion and fear:

> The idea of painless, non-threatening coercion is an illusion. Fear is the insepa-
> rable companion of coercion, and its inescapable consequence. (1964, p.175)

The fear Holt talked about was the fear children had of 'failing, of disappointing or displeasing the many anxious adults around them' (1964, p.9). In accordance with descriptions given by children themselves, 'fear' could mean: feeling scared, worrying, feeling pressured, dreading things, being uncomfortably tense, panicking and nervousness.

Fear in the classroom where knowledge is seen to be constructed, not transmitted, is a worrying phenomenon for three reasons:

1. Fear can lead to the child's partial or complete retreat from, and/or resistance to, classrooms and any learning that is intended to occur there (Fisher, 2011; Moore, 2013).
2. Fear itself, when produced by more powerful others against one's will, can lead to students taking fewer risks in their learning, being less creative, less inquiring, less outspoken and being less critical than otherwise (Flink et al., 1990; Ryan and Deci, 2000; Lemke et al., 2011).
3. Experiences of fear in classrooms can continue to have negative effects on the individual's confidence, sense of self and willingness to learn in the future (Southgate, 2003; Armstrong, 2006).

Children's descriptions of fear in the classroom
Introduction
In light of the importance of addressing fear for these three reasons, in the research project I describe below, I hoped to establish whether fear was perceived by pupils to be a common feature in one year 3 and one year 6 classroom; and if so, how it manifested itself and how children dealt with it.

The research was carried out in Meadowbank Primary School just outside London. The head teacher of the school, and especially the teachers of the two classes involved, believed that classrooms should be fun, supportive and creative places which would set pupils up for further learning in the future, especially self-directed learning which depended more on the learners' authority and less on the teacher's. The two classroom teachers made special efforts to help children to draw on their autonomy and self-direct their learning, in collaboration with peers. This progressive approach permeated both the classes I observed where pupils' affective needs were attended to, their social relationships were valued and their physical well-being prized. The two classrooms I observed seemed to be happy, inclusive, interactive places with children sitting in groups with whom they worked collaboratively. Both teachers appeared to care very much about the overall well-being of the children in their classes and the pupils seemed to respond affectionately to them.

In many ways, then, children's learning as knowledge-construction and meaning-making in these two classrooms seemed to stand a good chance of thriving. However, the way the school was run, as directed by government, was in tension with some of these two teachers' aims. Despite the rich opportunities offered by these two teachers, some vestiges of authoritarianism seemed to linger in the school to the detriment of the pupils' learning. It was these lingering vestiges of authoritarian approaches that led pupils to describe multiple occasions of worrying, dreading, panicking, feeling tense and pressured and in short, feeling (as pupil Mary put it) 'really, really scared'.

I interviewed 28 pupils, evenly divided among year 3 and year 6 pupils, and I observed four lessons in each of their two classrooms (eight lessons in total). I also collected written sentence-completions from all 60 children across both classes.

Children's fear and its influence on learning

The year 3 teacher, Miss Thorn, acknowledged immediately how fearful her pupils could be. Describing Carl, she commented: 'He's so fearful of everything all the time'. I asked her, 'So what would his worst nightmare in the classroom be?' and her reply was:

> Coming in and not having a clue what was going on. And then not being able to do it, and being criticised for not doing it right ... If they did that to Carl, he would probably run away and never come back.

About another pupil, Anna, she noted:

> She really worries about everything. She doesn't like that she finds things tricky. She's fearful of some of the other children on her table. She's fearful of upsetting Jill [the Teaching Assistant]. She's fearful of upsetting me.

Laila in year 3 noticed how fear got in the way of learning in the classroom. She advised teachers that: 'I think it helps you better when you're not scared'. For example, some of the pupils commented that when afraid:

> I lose my confidence and mess up my learning.
>
> You're too busy thinking about what has happened and there is not enough room in your head for learning.
>
> I won't be as involved in the lesson as normal.

Sapphire (year 6) expressed that feeling of forgetting everything through fear ('Forget Everything And Run, or F.E.A.R.', to use words from Watkins, 2013) and feeling very small (see Figure 2.1). The children seemed to think that concentration was the first victim of classroom fear, followed by reduced or alternatively excessive energy and consequently poor writing skills. One year 6 pupil said that, when anxious, he had to keep going out of class to get a glass of water to help him concentrate, but even then 'My head spins'. Anna (year 3) felt like giving up when she felt afraid: 'It feels like you have hit a brick wall because you don't want to go any further'. Too much of such fear-induced behaviour, many of them concluded, could lead to poor quality work.

Teacher Mrs Wesley noted the very scenario described by Holt, that pupils feared to let down the adults around them:

> ❛ I think they don't want to fail in *my* eyes. [Mrs Wesley, year 6 teacher] ❜

Having a strong relationship with the teacher is an important aspect of the productive classroom and Mrs Wesley clearly had a close connection with her pupils. However, doing tasks to please the teacher rather than for the value of learning them implies obedience rather than autonomy in the children's approach and suggests compliance rather than criticality. As Holt also suggested, this fear of upsetting adults could be even stronger than fear of physical punishment because the pupil makes the pressure their own and takes the blame for failure. And learning (or performing) to please the teacher can make the child more dependent on the teacher. For example, Peter (year 6) seemed to consider his challenge to be to impress the teacher: he claimed this was why he liked to read his work out in class. This suggested a dependence that might not have been helpful in his developing a learning orientation (as opposed to a performance orientation; see Chapter 3).

It appeared that other systems within the wider school could make teachers seem even more frightening. For example, the school used a punishment system of yellow and red warning 'cards' for poor behaviour. If pupils got awarded the red card, pupils had to speak with the deputy head teacher or the head teacher herself, both of whom the pupils apparently found scary. Another classroom-based punishment that pupils described as scary was being kept in at lunchtime. Being kept away from friends could make pupils both fearful and resentful towards the teacher and the school – and probably did not support their blossoming social identities. Peter (year 6) gave quite a dramatic account of how he believed isolation affected him:

> ❛ I think the only times when I feel scared *and* tense is when I'm told in the first lesson 'You're staying in at lunch,' so then I have like several other lessons to go through worrying about that, so I think that's a really bad thing … I just feel like collapsing. ❜

What I noticed in this study was the pupils' apparently constant fear of the teachers' surveillance. They seemed to feel that they should be working hard and understanding correctly all the time. They had very little freedom to take things easy, even when other important aspects of their life became difficult such as playground or home relationships. A slip in their attention risked causing a teacher to disapprove. Perhaps most worrisome was the fact that some children were scared that the teacher would be angry if they did not know the answer to a question. This was despite the inquiry-based approach preferred by both class teachers. Miss Thorn narrated how Mary (year 3) went to pieces if she thought she had got anything wrong:

> If I wrote a comment in her book, like 'Please can you try and put in your capital letters and full stops,' something like that, she would burst into tears, because she would take it really personally that she had failed.

Carl (year 3) revealed that he did not ask the teacher any questions when he perceived that she was tired because he guessed that she might become cross more quickly than usual. Many children in this study admitted being scared by teachers' shouting. They believed that they would be better off if teachers talked quietly and approached them individually to talk. Perhaps this fear was at the back of their consciousness whenever they did something that the teacher might not like. Mrs Wesley said that she tried not to shout at year 6 because she felt children learnt more when they were not afraid. However, the teacher in the next-door classroom made Mrs Wesley's class scared when they heard her shouting at another class through the wall. Mr Omer, deputy head teacher, was clearly feared by many pupils. Jem (year 6) explained why Mr Omer was scary like a tiger:

> You have to keep eye contact with it, otherwise it pounces on you.

The year 3 children seemed more frightened of the shouting of the head teacher. Mary (year 3) re-enacted for me the scenario of meeting the head teacher in the corridor by demonstrating the scream of fear she would give because of being 'freaked out' by the head's shouting. Nearly all the interview children recommended to teachers not to shout if they wanted children to learn well. Jem (year 6), for example, advised:

> If you're telling someone off, don't be all shouty and everything. Because ... if there's shouting, you kind of get scared.

Fear of being shouted at led to destructive habits such as pupils not daring to answer or ask a question and fearing to admit being unsure or wrong in front of the teacher. In short, the children tended to avoid risks and failed to trust their own judgements because they were inhibited by the judgements of teachers.

Related to their sense of a 'normal' and expected way of being in the classroom, which did not always make sense to them, the research revealed another fear: fear of not knowing quite how to be or what to do in the classroom. Year 3 children described how this fear manifested itself when:

> I don't think I can do it and I don't believe in myself.
>
> I am rubbish at something and I don't feel confident.

Harris (year 3) described how his colleague Carl would blush and stay very still when he felt this debilitating fear. Andrew and Norbert (year 6) recognised this sense of fear in other people whom they pitied, strongly reflecting the words of Southgate (2003; above) who noted how in fear, pupils tended to feel powerless and isolated. These two boys related their fear to the inflexible rules of the class-room but did not dare to challenge these:

> **Andrew:** When the teacher says to someone, 'Stand up!' it's someone who's about to cry because they're not doing it right. I really want to just break the rules and help them ...
>
> **Norbert:** When that's you, it's worse, because nobody can help you. You feel like you're trapped in a bubble.

Among several others, Clare and Jerry in year 3 claimed that they found it harder to learn when it was silent in the classroom and Carl even found it 'creepy'. Their discomfort, they explained, stopped them from concentrating on learning. Laura, a year 6 pupil, explained:

> You feel like really lonely ... I know there's, like, people around you, but it just feels like they're not really there. It's just – like there's a lot of tension in the air when it's like that.

This frequently expressed aversion to silence greatly surprised me because of the commonplace insistence on silence in most classrooms and my own prefer-ence for studying in a silent attic. Yet, among 21st-century children, silence is perhaps less common than it used to be. Silence is mainly a legacy from the traditional classroom in which the teacher would dominate *over* pupils' voices rather than encourage them to use and explore their *own* voices. It seems that silence might unwittingly be still over-used in some classrooms with negative effects for pupils.

This case study has illustrated how fear can interfere with pupils' learning even when their teachers support a conception of learning as knowledge-construction and meaning-making. This seemed, in this case, to be because there were remaining elements of an authoritarianism approach in their school (related to a traditional conception of learning) which hindered their learning: such as being shouted at by other teachers; being tightly surveyed all the time; being isolated from friends; and (sometimes) being silenced in the classroom.

Children's words: children's classroom fears in a country ridden with fear

In a war-torn country, Palestine, Saida Affouneh and I carried out research into the experiences of children in two primary schools (Affouneh and Hargreaves, 2015; Hargreaves and Affouneh, 2017). Our aim was to investigate the role of fear in the Palestinian classroom where authoritarian teaching was the norm. We were also intrigued to see what children's classroom experiences of fear were in a country where fear was widespread in everyday life. For example, some pupils faced violent threats simply by coming to school. In one school, there had been a murder on the doorstep of the actual school the night before our classroom observation. What was so striking was that, despite this external fear, the fears described by the pupils within the classroom were fears linked to the authoritarian nature of the class-room, with little reference to outside fears. In fact, many of the fears these pupils mentioned were similar to the fears explained by children in Meadowbank School (see section above).

We observed classes in one boys' school and one girls' school in a town named Ramallah and invited the children in both classes to complete some sentence-starters for us and to draw a picture of their classroom. We then selected five boys and five girls for individual interview and we interviewed their teachers. Their words were translated from Arabic into English.

Children's fears

The classes we observed in Ramallah were set out in the traditional way with indi-vidual desks facing the teacher at the front who stood near the blackboard. Silence was the norm during lessons and the teacher tended to do most of the talking in the traditional style. Despite political attempts to reform their classrooms to foster a more constructivist approach to learning, reform was slow to erode the deeply-ingrained habits of the traditional classroom.

There were a few children in the Ramallah schools, including some girls, who claimed never to feel fear at school. It appeared that they had learnt that fear was unacceptable and perhaps this approach had been learnt from the political situa-tion. One shocking picture drawn by a pupil called Jamila showed the girls' teacher telling the class: 'Read the board, or I will make you cry!' Bilal, Jamila's friend, appeared afraid of the teacher, in the picture; but Jamila was saying: 'No Bilal, don't be scared. Fear makes you weak.'

In the girls' school, the girls seemed particularly fearful of the school principal, for example, when she shouted at them in assembly. Indeed, both the boys' and the girls' teachers admitted that they deliberately used the principal as a threat with which to frighten the children into subservience. This seems to be a practice com-mon in many countries, including England.

Like the children in Meadowbank Primary School, in the Palestinian classrooms both girls and boys described how they feared being asked a question in public when they were not expecting it. This relates to the idea of visibility being fearful in a social atmosphere of judgement (Foucault, 1978). These pupils feared having to face dozens of other children and the teacher, and feared having to risk exposing their weaknesses. This was especially bad if they did not understand the teacher's question properly. They told us that in that case they felt a sense of shame and then panicky fear for not knowing what the teacher wanted (which also resonated with the research in Meadowbank).

Like the children in the UK school, both girls and boys described being frightened by teachers' shouting, although in the Ramallah schools it was their own classroom teacher who shouted (Figure 2.2). In one picture, a girl pupil illustrated feeling scared that the teacher would swear at her. Others were frightened generally if the teacher was angry or upset with the class, but at the same time they did not seem to question the teacher's right to become angry. This was despite the fact that the girls'

Figure 2.2   The scary teacher, drawn by year 5 pupils (Hargreaves and Affouneh, 2017)

teacher, Ahlam, told us that she was trying to maintain a more amicable rapport with her students, as required by recent reform directives. She told us: 'I don't shout at them or hit them, I just try to have good relations with the girls.' However, later she admitted that: 'Sometimes they drive me mad so I shout at them.'

Physical intimidation was harder for us to explore because it was completely outlawed by school policy. The boys' teacher, Mohammed, therefore probably felt obliged to tell us that he did not hit the boys with the stick. However, he also added that if the class were 'out of control, then we have to [hit them]. But we don't do this to children unless they hit each other'. He did also tell us he would smack them with his hand, even when he could not use the stick. On the other hand, the pupils themselves described being beaten with the stick. They talked about the fear of being beaten and fear of their peers being beaten. During beatings, they seemed to have been punished both through the experience of feeling fear and then by the physical pain itself. It is also notable that they felt their friends' pain too. Pupil Dani told us, for example:

> I don't like him hurting my friends. I worry about them.

He explained that being beaten himself was very painful; then he concluded thoughtfully: 'I learn best when the teacher is not angry.' In his interview, on the other hand, male pupil Farouk blamed his peers for the beatings: 'If they stop shouting, then he will not beat us.' In other words, he was emphasising his duty rather than his rights, which is a common occurrence in authoritarian systems. He had bought into the values and regulations of the authoritarian system.

Both boys and girls in the Ramallah schools reported fear of the 'normalising judgement' in relation to the exams. They vividly described the fear of finding the exam difficult. The prominence of the exam seemed to give the teacher more power to intimidate them. Children were afraid of making silly mistakes and also of not finishing the exam. And then there was the terror of waiting for the exam results to be delivered, the dread of not getting full marks and the fear of not being top of the class. According to a boy pupil, his teacher threatened to tell parents if boys did not perform well in class or in exams. This threat drew on the children's fear of disappointing – or infuriating – anxious adults at home as well as at school. Four girls actually drew pictures of their mothers being angry after they had not done well in class or in exams. The atmosphere of social judgement that accompanied the authoritarian approach therefore extended beyond the classroom walls and even beyond the school.

The influence of fear on learning

We invited the pupils from the two Ramallah schools to describe in writing what happened to their learning when they were experiencing fear in the classroom. Several pupils simply wrote that they could not learn when they were afraid. Two separate pupils wrote 'My brain stops'. As expressed also by the children in the UK classroom, concentration was clearly a key casualty of fear in the Ramallah classrooms. Pupils told us:

> I can't listen carefully.
>
> I pretend that I am listening.
>
> I stop learning and cry.

Some pupils described how the flow of their learning was interrupted by fear:

> I become hesitant.
>
> I slow down.
>
> I am disturbed.

Others described their reactions being *speeded up* in a debilitating way:

> My heart beats very fast.
>
> My hand shakes.
>
> I write very quickly.

Ultimately such reactions tended to lead them to get wrong answers and to forget 'everything' (their word!).

We asked the 60 pupils in this study about ways they knew to overcome fear in the classroom. Some pupils said that they tried to push fear away by shutting it out. For example, one child wrote: 'I put my head on the floor and don't listen to anything'. Others told us: 'I put my hands over my ears', 'I shut my eyes' and 'I sit very quietly and don't move'. Ten children said that they would pray when they felt afraid. Others described making themselves think about something nice when they were afraid, such as their families, homes and the pet cat. In all these cases, positive learning experiences were squeezed into the background. Only one child felt that fear encouraged her to 'Read and get involved in classwork'.

Children's accounts of learning without fear

Despite having little practice in metalearning reflection (see Chapter 3), some pupils in the Ramallah schools were articulate about different emotions that served their learning better than fear: enjoyment and personal involvement were the most important. For example, when asked to draw pictures of situations in which they learnt best, nearly one-third of the boys drew computers explaining that these were more fun and allowed them to learn more independently of the teacher and focus on what they were interested in. Other favoured subjects included art, singing, drama and story-telling. These turned out to be learning areas in which the pupils' creativity and meaning-making were encouraged, and in which the teacher had a less prescriptive role.

Two girls mentioned the value of *not* having to keep quiet in class: they wanted to be allowed to speak in class and ask the teacher questions whenever it would help them. Another girl pupil talked of the benefits of the teacher loosening her control by letting the pupils work things out on the board without being interrupted. In fact, as another respondent expressed it, they perceived that classroom learning happened most effectively when 'the teacher is not talking much'. Similarly, both the girls and the boys commented that they learnt best outside the classroom in more informal contexts where they could also talk with each other. That explained why more than one-third of the boys' pictures depicted learning situations in the open air, among trees, flowers and sunshine. This highlighted their perception that context was important for rich learning.

Summary comments

In these two schools, despite reform efforts, authoritarianism was more explicitly upheld than in Meadowbank school where knowledge-construction and meaning-making were constantly encouraged. What is noticeable, however, is that many of the fears expressed by the two nationalities were similar: fear of the teacher's wrath, fear of making a mistake, fear of being shouted at and fear of failing the dominant adults in their lives. How they responded to fear was also similar in that they tended to lose concentration and do less adequate work when they were afraid. These findings suggest that the authoritarian legacy dies hard and lives on despite different conceptions of learning and even in a country where there are other, more life-threatening sources of fear.

Defining authority in the classroom: when legitimate authority becomes coercive authoritarianism

The word 'authority' is sometimes used in everyday language as a synonym for force or coercive power. For example, 'He was the one with the authority: he had the military at his fingertips.' However, authority imposed via force or coercion can more accurately be defined as *authoritarianism* because it is founded on *coercion* rather than on *freely given consent* (Macleod et al., 2012).

Authority means a person having the right or the power to make decisions and have these acted on. Any person can have authority if they have that right or power: but what gives them the right or the power? What makes their right/power legitimate?

At the classroom level, *legitimate* authority implies that a teacher makes decisions, prescribes action and has their prescription responded to by her/his pupils, *within a context in which purposes and/or values are shared by teacher and pupils alike.* This means that the teacher and the pupils are all on the same route to somewhere valuable, and this is what makes the teacher's authority legitimate. For example, in everyday life, if we regard someone as an 'authority' about a topic, it usually means that we trust them to have a valuable and well-evidenced view on something and we are therefore likely to act on the advice they give us. It is in this sense that I refer to the teacher's legitimate authority. In other words, the benefit of the teacher's prescriptions must be evident to pupils because they believe that s/he has the pupils' best interests at heart. This current book is revealing that sometimes teachers' prescriptions are not seen as valuable by pupils and the coercion that teachers use to impose the prescriptions can become a source of aggravation.

A key basis for legitimising authority in the classroom is *professional knowledge or expertise.* That is, a teacher who has sound professional knowledge and/or expertise can be considered to be a legitimate authority in the classroom whose directives are worth listening to. Legitimacy could be earned through practical experience or through academic qualifications, depending on whether the system has an integrationist or a collectionist culture (Bernstein, 1971, p.47). Within the collectionist culture, where the transmission of traditional knowledge is valued over the construction of knowledge by students, legitimacy is likely to be based on academic qualifications, regardless of how skilled a teacher is pedagogically. In other cultures, the teacher's pedagogical expertise will provide that legitimacy as well as their academic qualifications (Holliday, 1994).

Where the legitimacy of the teacher's authority is drawn from her/his pedagogical or subject knowledge expertise, s/he attempts to *distribute* this authority among all children in the classroom. Her/his legitimacy is based on the assumption that authority is shared with 'apprentice' pupils as much as possible because the role of the teacher is to support others in becoming authoritative. The *authoritative* teacher, in contrast to the *authoritarian* teacher, therefore represents 'the impersonal authority of one who has himself [or herself] submitted to the discipline he [or she] wishes the child to acknowledge' (Nash, 1966, p.115). Rather than making others obey them, the authoritative teacher supports pupils to learn with and from them because the authoritative teacher has something valuable to distribute.

Locating the legitimacy of the teacher is crucial because, as suggested by Weber (1958, in Pace and Hemmings, 2006), where the authority figure is perceived as not legitimate, or where consent is not willingly given, then authoritarianism based on coercion is likely to dominate rather than authority based on legitimate expertise. Authoritarian leaders may coerce their subjects using:

- physical force (e.g. isolating pupils, making pupils extra visible, hitting);
- psychological control (e.g. shouting at pupils, threatening to become angry, threatening other negative consequences);

- exchange of incentives (e.g. giving pupils more playtime in exchange for hard work, talking about forthcoming exams as a reason to learn, promising promotion to a 'higher ability' group if a pupil works really hard); or
- persuasion (e.g. telling a pupil, 'Show me how clever you can be!' or 'Won't your mum be proud?').

The end result of any one of these is that a required response is given, *but without free consent*. John Holt (1964) pointed out that psychological coercion/control may be no less damaging than physical force. Indeed, it may be worse because it is less obvious. This is not to suggest that corporal punishment is desirable! It suggests rather that to a pupil, the pain of the wooden stick can be similar to (or even less than) the hurt caused, for example, by 'shouty' words, overly pressurising expectations or being categorised as 'less able'.

Roland Meighan and Clive Harber devised a hierarchy of authoritarian types from the 'autocratic' authoritarian to the 'consultant' authoritarian. However, they concluded that:

> [w]hile the degree of harshness and despotism within authoritarian schools varies from context to context and from institution to institution, in the majority of schools power over what is taught and learned, how it is taught and learned, where it is taught and learned, when it is taught and learned and what the general learning environment is like is not in the hands of pupils. (2007, p.238)

In other words, even the teacher who consulted her/his pupils may have been acting in an authoritarian way if s/he did not act on the feedback accrued from pupils. School Councils of pupils often exemplify this use of 'consultation' whereby only unimportant issues get discussed at the Council meetings and these are only acted upon if the head teacher agrees. For example, a young child explained:

> The teachers mostly decide things by themselves ... [A child] may suggest a proposal, but they [the teachers] don't choose that then, they choose their own proposal. (Thornberg, 2008, p.424)

In this case, despite being 'consultant', the teacher is expecting pupils to follow her/his own agenda even when they have made it clear that they do not sign up to it. Even though, therefore, teachers such as Miss Thorn and Mrs Wesley at Meadowbank School supported children to construct knowledge, make meaning and direct their own learning, ultimately the school still controlled 'what is taught and learned, how it is taught and learned, where it is taught and learned, when it is taught and learned and what the general learning environment is like'. Although many of the harsh aspects of an authoritarian approach were absent at Meadowbank, perhaps this aspect (giving pupils choice and allowing them to act on their own authority) is the most difficult currently to promote, given the authoritarian flavour of government policy in schools at present. Coercion by the school and the teacher (even in this sense of controlling all the decisions) can easily become sanctioned through the forces of habit, tradition or political motive. These conspire to make a coercive system accepted in classrooms even when it would be considered unthinkable elsewhere in society or among adults. The child's rights in the classroom somehow become an exception to normal social expectations and it is their dependence that gains emphasis instead.

Why authoritarianism?

The knowledge-transmitting classrooms of the past 5,000 years have celebrated the teacher as the dominant force, who at times would then become authoritarian when not all her/his students were willing to absorb knowledge in the way s/he prescribed. However, now that the knowledge-transmission conception of learning is challenged by nearly all educators, in favour of a constructivist theory of learning, why do authoritarian classrooms persist so tenaciously? Some ancient Christian doctrines have been suggested as one contributing factor (see p.25). Specifically political and economic factors as well as religious ones, however, seem to play a significant role in preserving the authoritarian tradition.

Henry Giroux (2005) has suggested that, despite the UK being a democratically governed country, undemocratic tendencies are tolerated – including in classrooms – because of the domination of big business in the UK. Giroux coined the phrase 'new authoritarianism' to describe the groups of people in democratic countries who tried to rise above the law and exploit others for commercial reasons. Nicola Pratt (2007) pointed out that exploitation through business is nothing new. It has been a central part of British colonialism over the past 500 years. The British elite has sometimes displayed ruthless authoritarianism as its colonial businessmen acted without regard to the wishes of people in foreign, resource-rich countries, using coercion to exploit their assets. Giroux's 'new authoritarianism' refers to the similarly ruthless drive for business people to make money today, this time sometimes within their own country. He suggested that legitimation of the *right to business* has led people to become immune to the suffering of those whom they oppress through it – with lack of empathy for other people being a key component of authoritarianism. Perhaps then authoritarianism in British classrooms is not as surprising as it first seemed, given both the history of the British ruling classes and the current dominance of neo-liberal business approaches in schools.

What is more, the snowballing effect increases: authoritarianism in classrooms makes students less likely to challenge authoritarianism itself. When the child is silenced in the classroom and taught obedience to authority by whatever means necessary, then the following is likely:

> Individuals repress their pain and rage only to have these surface later in life whether through oppression of others, or through the support of regimes or forces engaged in oppression. (Romanish, 1995, p.18, describing Miller (1983))

Where the teacher's authority assumes the form of authoritarianism in the school classroom, implying an underlying current of coercion and fear, or at least of tight control, it might be assumed that children come to accept coercion, fear and control as *acceptable* aspects of relationships between those with 'authority' and those without. The following examples from an inner-city London school demonstrate how certain individuals repressed their pain and rage against the controlling teacher by cultivating some crafty 'tricks' to thwart her.

Children's words: children's 'tricks' in classrooms as a way of combating an authoritarian culture

I suggested above that the teacher's control over pupils could be a source of strong negative feeling on the part of pupils. Laura Quick, teacher-researcher and MA student, carried out a study in an inner-city, multi-cultural London year 5 classroom. She investigated through a series of classroom observations and interviews how pupils experienced the teacher's control and rules there (Quick, 2015). Quick wrote that these children spoke about a number of tricks that they had learnt in order to deal with the (according to them) excessive control exercised by their teacher. These tricks consisted of the pupils appearing to do what they were told but actually doing something else. For example, one child was sent to the head teacher's office as a punishment but instead of going to his office, she wandered around the school for several minutes and then discretely returned to the classroom. Another example was pupils looking as though you had crossed your legs when sitting on the floor when in fact only one leg was crossed.

Quick described how it became apparent during her interviews that tricks gained their meaning and emotional significance within the context of the children's wider classroom experience of being controlled. A feeling of freedom at the successful execution of a trick was against a backdrop of experiencing themselves as generally controlled rather than autonomous in school. With the exception of Safa, a working-class boy pupil who excelled in everything, the children all said they felt 'bossed around' in school and that they did not like it. They depicted many features of an authoritarian approach in which the teacher tried to keep order over them, using coercion if necessary. A girl pupil, Lecia, told Quick:

> **Lecia:** It feels like – ... like you've been bossed around all the time.
>
> [*Whispering*] It feels so annoying!
>
> **Quick:** Can you talk so I can hear?
>
> **Lecia:** Oh. [*Louder*] It feels so annoying! [*Shouting*] I just want to break *free* and do whatever I want!

Shauna added:

❝ The teachers are like always telling us to do stuff, and I don't like it because sometimes teachers, yeah, like Desreta said last time, she said teachers are always controlling her, always telling her what to do. ❞

Desreta accorded:

❝ And I don't like getting bossed around ... but they always boss us around. And no one likes it. ❞

Lecia developed a rather sophisticated analysis of the nice feeling that tricks gave her in the context of feeling otherwise controlled, which gave added meaning to the concept of the 'normalising judgement' (Foucault, 1978; see above):

❝ **Lecia:** Because basically you're bossed around every – You're not standing out and being your own self. Because normally that happens to every single child.

Quick: What does?

Lecia: Being bossed around ... So then, normally, when you do your own thing [i.e. tricks] you kind of stand out a bit – from the crowd.

Quick: How is that, to stand out a bit from the crowd?

Lecia: You feel normal – and not just – ordinary and ... just being with the crowd all the time –. Like – you could be your own crowd [*begins singing*]!

Quick: So when you say it makes you feel normal?

Lecia: A different type of normal.

Quick: I'm trying to understand that.

Lecia: You've got normal as not standing out, just being with the crowd, and you've got normal as feeling yourself. Two different things.

Quick: And how do tricks help with the normal-feeling-yourself?

Lecia: Oh. Because you're doing your own thing! – You're not being – the same every day – you just do your own thing. You just feel quite happy because you're doing your own thing. And you're being yourself – a bit. ❞

The feelings of autonomy the children voiced in relation to their defiant tricks seemed to go hand in hand with feelings of competence. Michael, another pupil, commented about his mastery of tricks which defied the teacher:

❝ **Michael:** It makes me feel like I'm the cleverest boy in the whole school ... and that I can do anything I want!

Desreta: Miss Lyon says 'cross your legs' and you go like this [*demonstrates with one leg bent to look crossed from the teacher's chair, the other in front*].

Quick: So how does it – what are you thinking when you're doing that?

Shauna: We feel like – she doesn't know what we're doing – and we feel like, very clever.

Desreta: Yeah, clever, clever, clever, clever, because, because, definitely because we can use our brain. We can use our strength! It's a good feeling, it's a good feeling.

Shauna: Yeah! 'Cause we can control –. Every single time when we do tricks we control stuff. Like, we don't, we don't get told off because they think everything we say is true, so it feels like *we* control *them* [her emphasis], all the teachers. It feels – free!

Yancy: It makes me feel cleverer than the teacher because ... she doesn't even know that I'm laughing.

Michael: The king of the school!

Quick related how Michael had told her that he felt 'really proud' when he did a trick and did not get caught and Desreta said: 'I feel like "yeah, I've done it, I've done what I'm meant to do, like. I've, I've, I've – I've got the job done"'. Both were in the 'lowest' sets for maths and literacy, so for them tricks may have been considerably more likely to provide these feelings of pride than academic achievement routes.

The good feelings of autonomy and competence that came from successful execution of tricks were the most frequent and most motivated comments of all the interviews in Laura Quick's research. Desreta's words about school without tricks suggested how very important they were to her:

Quick: What would school be like if you did no more tricks, or you got caught for every one?

Desreta: We will never be caught for any of our tricks!

Quick: But if I had a magic wand? I'm trying to work out whether ...

Desreta: [*Interrupting*] Even if you used your magic wand we would still find –. Everywhere we can make tricks.

The little boy, Safa, was the only participant who seemed uninterested in and sometimes unaware of the tricks the other children spoke so passionately about. While many of them described tricks as providing a feeling of autonomy from the oppression they felt, several commented that Safa did not experience the same level of control by teachers. Desreta told Quick that Safa 'gets to do what he wants a lot' because teachers 'don't boss the clever children around'. The teacher, Miss Lotts, said that she had '*never ever* had to tell him off'. Shauna said: 'He's good and the teachers feel like he's the best and he should do whatever he wants'. Safa seemed to have a similar opinion:

> **Quick:** Safa, do you ever feel that the teachers control you too much in school?
>
> **Safa:** No.
>
> **Quick:** Do you feel like you get to do what you want?
>
> **Safa:** Well, if you know what they're going to ask – they don't really tell you because they probably expect you to know by now. It's like it's been pro-grammed into you – so like you've – picked it up along the way as they've been teaching throughout the year.

And he said that as a result of this:

> You're able to do stuff, and, and you can't be told, like, that you can't. She'll allow you to come into the classroom at lunchtime and play inside on the com-puter ... and she'll give you responsibilities. And sometimes Miss will go out the classroom so she trusts you to stay in the classroom [alone] and do a good job.

Lecia also felt this freedom to 'do stuff' was a reward for Safa 'already' knowing what to do:

> Miss doesn't really interfere with Safa because he already knows what he's doing. So he just basically does his own thing. He doesn't really get told much at all.

It is perhaps notable that for Safa, in contrast to Lecia, 'doing his own thing' meant doing what the school wanted rather than standing out from the crowd. After a discussion about whether tricks meant children felt less 'bossed around', Quick asked Safa if, for him, one of the advantages of being regarded as responsible and anticipating what the teacher wanted was that he was bossed around less, but he did not seem to fully understand the question. Lecia, however, interrupted to explain:

> **Lecia:** It's like two paths, but the two paths lead the same way. So for example, one path is trick lane, the other path is good lane and then the trick lane and good lane both lead to the same place, so either way you still find the area.
>
> **Quick:** And what's the area?
>
> **Lecia:** The area is 'you get to do what you want' lane [doing your own thing].

Laura Quick's interpretation, however, was that the 'you get to do what you want lane' was not as simple a destination as Lecia made it sound. Lecia may have viewed Safa as doing what he wanted, but he was also doing what the school wanted. Quick suggested that through the governmentality lens coined by Michel Foucault (1978), he was on his way to becoming a 'docile body': that is, a body that *chooses* to do as it should. He had been 'programmed' (to use his own word) so effectively that he no longer had to be told or observed; he had *submitted to the authority and values of the system* (Raby, 2012).

In summary, by far the most frequent reason given by the children for executing tricks was the positive feelings that resulted from doing so successfully, that is, without being caught. These seemed mainly to be feelings of autonomy and competence. Ironically, their tricks also displayed considerable initiative and self-direction. Quick suggested that there was a deeply-embedded notion among some of these pupils that this was the main motive for existing at school: trying to out-do the all-powerful teacher and thereby trying to improve one's status among other pupils. The complexity of life in the authoritarian classroom comes through clearly in Quick's study. It emphasised the reality that where pupils' autonomy in the classroom was overly limited, their classroom experience came to include significant elements of anger and desire leading to their energy being put into complex projects that were detached from formal curriculum learning.

Quick's findings chime with those of Helen Fisher's (2011) study in which she found that pupils spent a lot of time and energy in hiding the fact that they actually did not want to comply with the teachers and yet they felt they had to for fear of teachers' disapproval. Fisher described this as 'dissatisfaction behind a veil of compliance'. Although their dissatisfaction was expressed in perhaps less obvious ways than among the children in Laura Quick's class, the message was the same: they were not giving their voluntary consent to the rules and values imposed by their teachers but they were working hard on pretending to do so.

Freedom versus prescription in the classroom

Most of the children in Laura Quick's study seemed to blame the teacher for the lack of freedom they experienced. Paulo Freire's famous writings (1972, 1998) addressed teachers directly, inviting us to work *with* students towards a world where people felt free, rather than trying to *control* students and turn them into something that they were not. Freire held that authoritarian teachers aimed to change the consciousness of the children themselves to meet the teachers' own interests rather than striving *with* the children for *everyone*'s freedom – as would the *authoritative* teacher who valued social justice. However, he described the 'fear of freedom' of dominators (which could mean teachers) who, instead of pursuing freedom, sought to sustain the status quo so that they themselves could avoid trouble in the current system (1972, p.16). The oppressors therefore feared their own and others' freedom, for the sake of their own power.

By freedom, Freire meant a world where people felt both autonomous and related to others, 'a world in which it will be easier to love' (1972, p.19): in this world, people became 'more fully human' (p.21), reached towards 'human completion' (p.24) and no longer felt isolated from each other. As John Dewey claimed earlier in the 20th century (1938), freedom did not mean absence of controls but rather was embodied *in the means by which it was decided who had a voice and role* in governing. In the research described above, it seemed to be not just the controlling rules that the children spent their time fighting but also the fact that these rules were entirely in the control of the teacher.

Freire suggested that the authoritarian teacher played the role of 'depositor, prescriber, domesticator' – perhaps fitting descriptions of how Laura Quick's pupils seemed to experience their teacher. Freire proposed that infantile (dependent) rather than mature (autonomous) responsibility had become inscribed into the text of classrooms, as demonstrated by Safa, who had taken on board the school's responsibilities not through his own initiation and negotiation but submissively. Schools try to induce this dependent responsibility through systemic emphasis on 'punctuality, quiet orderly work in groups, response to orders, bells and timetables, respect for authority, even tolerance of monotony, boredom and punishment, lack of reward and regular attendance' (Nash, 1966).

Children expend effort on meeting these organisational requirements rather than on more valuable aspects of learning. The children in Laura Quick's study (above) did show a great deal of initiative and self-direction in carrying out their tricks, in order not to meet requirements; but the energy they spent on doing so could have been directed towards more appropriate learning goals. Alternatively, these children could have resorted to physical violence if their frustrations grew unmanageable and perhaps later in secondary school they would do this. This would be made more likely because they had already learned from the primary classroom that using coercion to control others is the normal way to behave and respond. Rebecca Raby argued that the inherently gendered, racialised, class-based nature of school rules ran the risk of implementing an authoritarianism rather than democratic regime if the school rules were 'not critically assessed, discussed and debated within and outside of school settings' (Caron, 2014, p.305, describing Raby, 2012). School rules fostered compliance through threat of punishment, without child input into the matters that concerned them the most.

When children are thought of as authoritative about what helps their learning rather than just as compliers, they can be understood as social actors shaping as well as shaped by their environment. This is by no means an easy duality for teachers to manage, but it seems to be exactly what the children in the case study above were asking for. When the duality feels too difficult, the adult is inclined to 'ignore the interdependency that necessarily characterises all social relations and, instead, to underscore children's dependency on them as both "natural" and "inherent"' (James, 2011, p.177). This perceived dependency and reliance that are attributed to children have been used to legitimise tight boundaries within the ideologies of 'care and protection'. In other words, the care and protection of children provide a legitimation for emphasising that children are dependent and that they need to be controlled, rather than allowing them to take risks or exercise their own authority – which is more challenging for the caring teacher.

However, the vulnerability of young children cannot be confused with an inability to think and to act for themselves but on a more positive note can be seen as an opportunity for inducting them into empathetic ways of relating to others (see Saevi, 2015; Chapter 1). According to Jean Rudduck and Michael Fielding, a child is both autonomous and dependent: 'her/his autonomy is not diminished by the condition of being a child who also relies on adults' and this complexity needs to be embraced rather than evaded (2006, p.225). Likewise, Freire concluded that the solution was not to integrate children into the structure of oppression, but rather to transform that structure so that children could become authoritative for themselves (1972, p.48). In the interim, children would be key players in the process of that transformation towards a less oppressive structure. This partnership was what Freire, among others, saw as the opposite of oppression: where teachers and children became jointly responsible for a process in which all grew, where the vertical hierarchy of the classroom was broken down and where people taught each other, 'mediated by the world' (p.53). The educational process, he said, meant 'overcoming authoritarianism' so that the system resulted in the humanisation of all players.

ACTIVITIES FOR CLASSROOM PRACTICE: SOME PRACTICAL WAYS FORWARD FOR TEACHERS AND OTHER EDUCATORS IN CLASSROOMS

Discussion or journal writing

With a partner or in a private learning journal, describe your reactions to the children's voices cited in this chapter. In particular consider their comments about:

- the difference between authority and authoritarianism;

- how authoritarian practices can hinder learning and well-being;

- children's fear in the classroom;

- the importance of relatedness to the teacher; and

- alternatives to an authoritarian approach.

What did you find surprising?
What can be learned from these examples for classroom practice with children?

Actions to try out

Try asking pupils to keep a private record of times when they felt fear in the class-room. Give pupils dedicated time to do this and perhaps model some answers based on your own experiences as a pupil in the past. Allow pair talk about pupils' responses, stressing that they need only share as much as they feel comfortable with sharing.

When these records have been kept for a while, invite pupils' suggestions for reducing or dealing productively with fear in the classroom. Try having two lists: 1) What pupils could do differently to reduce their fear; and 2) What teachers could do differently to reduce pupils' fear.

Plenary

Describe, reflect on and analyse for yourself or in a pair/group, what happened when these actions were tried out in classrooms.

How will you engage pupils in evaluating any of the ideas you have tried out?

3

Autonomy in the classroom

> **Dave:** If I ask for help, I need help, but most of the time I come up with stuff on my own.
>
> **EH:** Yes. So how does that make you feel when she [the teacher] does it for you?
>
> **Dave:** I'm not sure. Probably – I'm not sure what it's called, but someone has the idea, and you just write it down for them – it's weird.
>
> **EH:** You end up feeling like a —?
>
> [*Long pause*]
>
> **Dave:** Postman.
>
> **EH:** Postman?
>
> **Dave:** Yeah, because they have to deliver letters. (Dave, year 5)

Chapter 3 explores pupils' descriptions of feeling autonomous and how these experiences relate to classroom learning conceived as knowledge-construction and critical meaning-making. That means, the chapter investigates whether or how pupils come to believe in and act on their own right and power to make decisions for learning in and about the classroom. The chapter provides examples of occasions when children had a sense of autonomy and had the opportunity to exercise this, in contrast to situations where the authoritarian classroom inhibited it. The chapter draws for its 'Children's words' on qualitative studies from two English primary school classrooms as well as from a large research project among primary pupils learning English as a second language in Alexandria, Egypt. The seminal works of both John Dewey (1899) and Ryan and Deci (2000) are emphasised in this chapter.

Autonomy

The autonomy-promoting teacher helps pupils develop their sense of self in relation to others, and to act accordingly. The autonomy-promoting teacher lays the foundations for children coming to believe in their own authority: to believe in and act on their own right and power to make decisions for learning in and about the classroom. Taking the opposite of an authoritarian approach to the classroom, the autonomy-promoting teacher distributes her/his control over pupils *among* those same pupils by allowing them to exercise genuine choices and mature responsibilities in their learning, based on their own authority. S/he thereby aims to promote shared authority in the classroom.

'Autonomy' is a much over-used word that means substantially different things to different users. I still employ the word here because no other word quite conveys an equivalent meaning. 'Proactive engagement, self-direction and critical reflection' perhaps gets closest. It may be useful to clarify straight away what I do *not* mean by autonomy.

Autonomy does *not* mean:

- *Students working in isolation.* An autonomous child feels in control of what s/he is doing, regardless of where s/he is placed in relation to others. In fact, the best classroom collaboration may come about only when all participants feel autonomous rather than dependent on others.

Autonomy does *not* mean:

- *Students working silently without asking questions.* The autonomous learner is likely to ask plenty of questions in order to acquire the information or feedback that they need for their desired learning. Dialogue with others is likely to be helpful in the learning of the autonomous learner. As Little (1991, p.7) pointed out, 'Autonomy is not a synonym for self-instruction ... it is not limited to learning without a teacher ... it does not entail an abdication of responsibility on the part of the teacher.'

Autonomy does *not* mean:

- *Students having a free reign, doing what they like.* There is a misconception that a teacher who allows her/his pupils to be autonomous allows children to do what they like. Children are legally obliged to take an education (in most places), so a legal limit to a free reign in terms of attendance is already in place. Behaviour inside the classroom must also be ordered so that everyone is free and equal, especially while the current schooling model places 30 or more pupils with one teacher. However, order can be sustained in a range of ways and by a range of people, some of which allow and encourage more autonomy than others.

I suggest that autonomy in the classroom *does* mean that learners:

- start to realise, express and act on their own preferences and the strategies that help them;
- feel less dependent on adults or others to achieve and to set goals;
- ask for help when and in the way that will most support them;
- take initiatives and decisions in and about their learning where suitable;
- see learning as a collaborative enterprise in which their own voice is valuable; and/or
- become critically aware of their contexts and their power to change contexts.

This book refers frequently to the self-determination theory of Ryan and Deci because their emphasis on the essential and inseparable trio of competence-autonomy-relatedness seems particularly useful when considering the whole experience of the child's learning in the classroom and the nurturing of learning autonomy. Ryan and Deci, in their seminal (2000) work, explained self-determination theory in terms of a *critical distinction* between volitional and controlled behaviours:

> We have briefly presented self-determination theory in order to make the critical distinction between behaviors that are volitional and accompanied by the experience of freedom and autonomy—those that emanate from one's sense of self—and those that are accompanied by the experience of pressure and control and are not representative of one's self. (p.65)

This description hints at the problems of classroom experiences characterised by pressure and control, as illustrated in the previous chapter (Chapter 2). The difference between those classroom experiences and experiences where the pupil has a sense of freedom and autonomy is that in the latter experiences, the pupil has a stronger sense of self. As Lecia put it in Laura Quick's research (see Chapter 2 for the whole interview), this means:

> You're doing your own thing! You're not being the same every day. You just do your own thing. You just feel quite happy because you're doing your own thing. And you're being yourself.

Ryan and Deci (2000) went on to spell out the connections between classroom tasks, autonomy and the learner's sense of competence (i.e. their sense of being capable):

> *Cognitive Evaluation Theory* (CET) ... which is considered a subtheory of self-determination theory, argues that interpersonal events and structures (e.g. rewards, communications, feedback) that conduce toward *feelings of competence* during action can enhance intrinsic motivation for that action because they allow satisfaction of the basic psychological need for competence ... CET further specifies that feelings of competence will *not* enhance intrinsic motivation unless they are accompanied by *a sense of autonomy* or, in attributional terms, by an *internal perceived locus of causality*. (p.58)

This final statement has far repercussions if taken seriously: *feelings of competence will not enhance intrinsic motivation unless they are accompanied by a sense of autonomy.* In other words, when children achieve something in the classroom, it will not encourage them to continue learning unless they feel that they had some choice in learning it. In order for a sense of competence to inspire the child to keep learning, they must appreciate the value of the task and they must willingly give their consent to doing it. This is also the basis for children experiencing the teacher as an *authority* rather than as an *authoritarian* (see Chapter 2 for a detailed explanation of this). Coercion through rewards, punishments, exchanges or persuasions will not substitute the learner's sense of autonomy.

This statement, that *feelings of competence will not enhance intrinsic motivation unless they are accompanied by a sense of autonomy* undermines the assumption that imposed learning targets and imposed tasks are effective for meaningful learning! It is an essential wake-up call to all educators to nurture the kind of relationship with our students in which the purposes of doing tasks and meeting targets are reflected upon and negotiated: to allow learners to decide whether to sign up to them or not. If not, then, according to Ryan and Deci, success is unlikely.

The autonomous learner, who gains competence by choice, could be described as the proactively self-directed learner, in the sense that their driving wheel is within themselves and they choose to use it (what Ryan and Deci called an 'internal perceived locus of causality'). Paulo Freire, whose whole philosophy was based on the idea of actualising human autonomy, thereby encouraged students to become autonomous by *moving from* being:

- spectators *to* actors;
- followers of prescriptions *to* makers of choices;
- silent *to* outspoken. (1972, p.25)

These three transformations represent the move from carrying out tasks because one has been told to, and carrying them out because one believes in them and has chosen to act in a particular way for valuable reasons. Autonomy (or proactive engagement and self-direction with critical reflection) suggests creating or controlling a situation by taking an informed initiative, rather than waiting for things to be done *for* you or *to* you. Autonomy ultimately allows individuals thereby to enjoy 'full social engagement and participation' (Marmot, 2004, p.2) rather than acting as spectators or consumers. This participation includes the capacity for critiquing social processes. Marginalised groups such as pupils from families with lower socio-economic status may be excluded from such participation because their autonomy has been undermined by unjust social structures (see Chapter 5).

Alfie Kohn in his chapter 'A classroom of their choosing' (1996) explored the issue of teacher control in contrast to pupils' autonomy, making the case for children having a greater *say* in classrooms to enrich their learning. He observed a teacher in Southern California who effected positive change when she stopped commanding so much and listened to the learners in the classroom. Kohn stressed that working *with* children would always create better conditions for learning than teaching that was based around rewards or punitive measures handed down by the teacher. He stated: 'If we want children to take responsibility, we must give them responsibility and plenty of it' (p.84). He argued that children who were allowed greater volition in the classroom became more committed to decision making. In addition, less controlling teachers helped to develop learners who were more interested in learning for their own sake and therefore engaged more enthusiastically with it. Kohn recognised that allowing or encouraging such volition in the classroom was not easy for teachers because they themselves were constrained by external pressures and may therefore unwittingly muffle learners' voices and limit their choices. He commented:

> Researchers have discovered when teachers are pressured to improve students' performances on tests, they tend to act in more controlling ways with students, giving them less choice than do teachers who are free to facilitate students' learning. (p.100)

Deci et al. (1981) suggested that when children learn out of curiosity and have the desire to challenge themselves, this can result in a greater involvement and satisfaction with their learning, allowing them to integrate and understand learning material more fully. These ideas are in keeping with key learning theorists such as Piaget, Vygotsky and Bruner. They proposed that autonomy developed in classrooms when teachers encouraged pupils to engage in:

- lessons that allow for student initiative and/or decision making;
- inquiry-based tasks providing opportunities for exploration, taking risks/making mistakes;
- activities that draw out pupils' natural curiosity (intrinsic motivation);
- collaboration/interaction with teachers/other students;
- critical reflection and/or metalearning.

Based on the writing of the authors above, autonomy in learning can be defined as constituting two complementary halves:

- pupils' proactive engagement and self-direction; and
- their critical inquiry and comment.

Put differently, the autonomous learner:

- can act inter-dependently with external authority and take the initiative for thinking and then acting as s/he sees fit;
- senses an equal right to explore and express their own particular views, free from others' inhibiting judgements, and therefore has the competence to challenge habitual ways of thinking and traditional notions about her/his position in learning and/or in life.

If all school pupils became autonomous in these ways, Schiro's (2013) last two purposes for state education would probably be met:

- the growth of individuals: his or her own unique intellectual, social, emotional and physical attributes; and
- the development of a critically educated citizenry able to engage reflectively and reflexively with the wider society.

Autonomy as proactive engagement and self-direction

John Dewey, presenting in USA in 1899, expressed strikingly relevant messages for today, in relation to a child developing their sense of self in the classroom. He criticised the uniformity of the 'ordinary schoolroom, with its ... desks almost all of the same size' (see Chapter 1), but promoted the uniqueness of each child's action: 'The moment children *act* they individualise themselves; they cease to be a mass, and become the intensely distinctive beings that we are acquainted with out of school ... we do not find that [the child] is first of all a listening being; quite the contrary' (pp.15–16; my emphasis).

Dewey went on to decry teachers' practice of 'modelling', popularly acclaimed as a useful resource in today's UK classrooms. Dewey suggested that no activity should be *originated* by imitation and that the start must come from the child's curiosity and initiative: 'The model or copy may then be supplied in order to assist the child in imaging more definitely what is it that [s/]he really wants – in bringing him [her] to consciousness' (pp.28–9). Dewey warned that if the child was pressured by the teacher's models, s/he would become 'servile and dependent, not developed' in which case the teachers' models performed as 'external, arbitrary impositions interfering with normal growth'. These are strong reminders of the need to allow children the space for expressing curiosity and taking initiatives in the classroom, despite the pressures on teachers to 'deliver' standardised outputs.

It is important to emphasise that autonomy as proactive engagement and self-direction can thrive hand in hand with collaborative interaction. Autonomy in the sense of initiative-taking is in fact an important part of genuine collaboration, which may seem counter-intuitive to some people. Contributing successfully within an interactive community, according to Michael Fielding, demanded that each person's part was *original and whole in itself* (Fielding, 1996). The learning community did not consist of 'herds of an identical animal' all copying the teacher's model, but of diverse contributors making unique but valuable contributions, including the teacher's. This in itself is a reflection of each person's autonomy. Fielding rejected the idea of the 'organic' whole whereby each part of the whole only functioned to make the whole work. For example, each part of a car depended on all key other parts of the car to make the car work. In terms of autonomy, however, being part of the community meant providing one's own enterprising contribution which ultimately would benefit the whole *but was not dependent on the whole nor the whole on it.* In this sense, autonomy depended on each person having both an equally valued contribution and the freedom to share this or not, as those in the community learnt collaboratively together. As an outcome of this process of equality and freedom, equal and free relationships could be fostered through which further learning would be enriched.

As discussed at length in Chapter 4, autonomy in the sense of the child's proactive engagement and self-direction can be restricted or encouraged depending on a teacher's feedback. The extent to which any child is willing to take risks and make mistakes depends partly on this. Harry Torrance and John Pryor (1998) described a spectrum from convergent to divergent assessment and feedback (see Chapter 4). In providing convergent feedback, often within the tradition of the closed initiation response feedback (IRF) cycle, the teacher might confirm, reject or elaborate on a child's response as feedback (the 'F' part of IRF). This feedback might help the learner to follow certain steps in order to complete a task. However, although this allows for the pupil's independent action as a response to feedback, it does not allow for initiative-taking, nor proactive engagement nor critical inquiry, and therefore it is of limited use in autonomy promotion. Torrance and Pryor suggested that divergent rather than convergent feedback was likely to benefit children's initiative-taking in the classroom more, in the form of exploratory or provocative feedback rather than descriptive or directive feedback. Provocative feedback could lead to further (willing?) inquiry or exploration rather than just revision or correction.

Autonomy as pupils' critical inquiry and comment

John Pryor and Barbara Crossouard (2008) have emphasised the meta-social, critical capacity of the learner as a key aspect of autonomy. They described

> an explicit aim of raising students' critical awareness both of the discourses of the educational setting, and also of the wider social construction of these discourses ... The pedagogic texts and the teaching context therefore become the object of critique, rather than functioning to 'deliver' knowledge. (p.8)

These authors were emphasising that through critical reflection in the classroom, practised by pupils and teachers, autonomy in this further sense was both expressed and developed. In other words, people did not learn to be autonomous by fitting into someone else's system but by reflecting on and critiquing this system, including their own position within it. Dewey, similarly, proposed that the classroom was the microcosm of society and it was here that children became apprentices in exercising social power and insight:

> It is only where a narrow and fixed image of traditional school discipline dominates, that one is in any danger of overlooking that deeper and infinitely wider discipline that comes from ... *the development of social power and insight.* (Dewey, 1899, p.10; my emphasis)

An important part of developing social power and insight is through pupils critiquing the institution of the classroom rather than accepting 'the dictatorship of no alternatives' there (Unger, 2011). As described by Stephen Kemmis (2006), some educators considered this insight to be the job of the official 'authorities' because opening up a debate about classrooms among children could lead to children 'asking uncomfortable questions about the quality of education offered' (p.460). However, Kemmis went on to say that, in his view, this was precisely the task of the critical educator.

Autonomy is learnt rather than taught

In Harry Torrance's (2012) words, learners in classrooms operated more like apprentices than like slaves precisely because they had the capacity and preference for autonomy. In that sense, it was not direct instruction that would make the most difference to children's autonomy development but the community developed by the teacher in each classroom. One cannot coerce people to become autonomous. Parents sometimes notice that young children tend to behave, mainly unwittingly, how the parents *behave* rather than in line with what the parents *say*. This might be because deep down, young children want to become part of their parents' community and share their ways of doing things. By aiming to fit in with how their parents do things, they hope to feel a stronger sense of self in belonging to this community. This aim is more satisfying and meaningful to them than just following their parents' instructions, especially when these don't seem to make sense. On this assumption, the most successful way to encourage autonomy in the classroom is for the teacher to act autonomously her or himself, in both the ways listed above (i.e. by taking self-directed initiatives in teaching and by exercising critical reflection). In a classroom where the teacher values their own autonomy and the autonomy of the pupils, and where the teacher deliberately nurtures it in their comments and actions, the children in that class are likely to become autonomy apprentices whose autonomy is expressed and starts to grow within this community, regardless of (or despite) other school prescriptions or restrictions.

Children's words: pupils' critical inquiry and comment

In the section above, one key aspect of autonomy was theorised as 'critical inquiry and comment'. For children to exercise their autonomy, they need to practise critical inquiry and comment. McCallum et al. suggested in 2000:

> Important studies have shown that children across junior and secondary schools have views and opinions about teachers, teaching and the classroom climate, including the subtler aspects of negotiation and control of what counts as knowledge. As yet, however, few studies at primary level have collected the views of young children on learning. (p.278)

Many years later, this is still uncomfortably the case and pupils are sometimes aware of their limited opportunities to express their views in a genuine way. That was the main purpose for writing this book.

In 2012, I carried out a six-month long study with nine year 5 pupils in Emerald Primary School in Surrey (see Chapter 4). This involved interviewing children and asking them to talk about lessons they had just had. Their research names were Aaron, Dave, Esther, Farhana, Laila, Josh, Maddie, Mia and Vijay. At the end of the study I asked the nine participant pupils to reflect on their experience of being a participant in the study as a whole. One of the most frequent responses was that they appreciated being a valuable participant and having a meaningful *part to play*. All the children appreciated being asked their views, but some of them found it more difficult to be honest with me than others. For example, two of the girls, Laila and Farhana, explained how they had gradually grown more confident in being open with me as they got used to having interviews with me. Laila said that she had gradually learnt to 'tell the truth and not to keep it *bottled up*' [my emphasis]. Her colleague, Esther, admitted that she used to 'twist the truth' a bit to start with, until she realised that I *really* wanted to know what she thought. Mia and Farhana both said that they found all the interviews boring to start with, until they realised that actually, no bad consequences would occur if they were completely honest! They explained to me that they did not really expect to give their true opinion at school – which may explain why they sometimes found school boring too (see also Helen Fisher's (2011) work, regarding children hiding their true feelings at school behind a 'veil of compliance').

The idea that children are not asked their views about issues that affect them in the classroom was also reflected in our research study in Alexandrian primary schools among 394 ten-year-old Egyptian children (Hargreaves et al., 2016). In response to the question, 'How did you feel about participating in this research?' out of 394 pupils, 243 pupils talked about the joy, happiness and *sense of freedom* that resulted from the research team asking them their views about the classroom (see Sara's quotation at the start of Chapter 1, translated from the Arabic). Over 100 pupils stressed the value in actually being enabled to express their opinion in the classroom, about the classroom. For example, Samia told us:

> I can't refuse research like this as it gives me the freedom to write what I want.

Khadija referred to the fear that she normally associated with being questioned:

> I feel happy to participate with the adults. This is the first time someone has asked me about my opinion and asked me *not to be afraid* and trust myself. [My emphasis]

Ghada appreciated that her opinions were respected:

> I feel that you value my opinion: no one has ever listened to us. I would like to thank everyone who comes and respects our opinions.

In another school, Ossama explained:

> I feel that someone appreciates our opinions. Our teachers do not care about our opinions. They just pay us lip service and that's it. Thank you very much! You put a smile on my face [drawing of a smiley face]. I hope you will come again. I feel this is important. You made me feel that I am unlocking my potential.

Their sense of being proactive and free was tangible as they expressed now feeling a link to powerful people in powerful places such as the Ministry of Education and universities. For example, Moussa told us:

> I have a beautiful feeling because we have [with us in the classroom] professors from big universities such as Alexandria University and University of London.

Amr added:

> I am very happy because I take part in research with adults and they are professionals.

Forty-five of the pupils believed that by expressing their critiques they could make an impact more widely, and help to benefit other pupils who sometimes had difficult experiences in classrooms. Just one person, Hala, noted also that through this research there may have been a shift in power relations. Referring to the research team as 'the teachers' (which we were), she commented: 'The teachers are being humble with the pupils'. Perhaps there is a humility in adults seriously inquiring of pupils what their critiques are.

Metalearning is the key to autonomy

> The child should be given intellectual responsibility for selecting the materials and instruments that are most fit, and given an opportunity to think out their own model and plan of work, led to perceive errors and find out how to correct them. (Dewey, 1899, p.50)

In this exhortation, John Dewey was describing how autonomy might be manifested by children in the classroom through a process that has come to be known as metalearning (Watkins, 2015). In Chris Watkins' (2001) words:

> If learning is the process of creating knowledge by making sense of your experience, metalearning is the process of making sense of your experience of learning. (p.5)

By encouraging learners to critique what they have learnt, reflect on how they learnt it and *analyse what they have learnt about learning it*, they take the driving seat in their own learning. In Ryan and Deci's (2000) language, such pupils rely on an internal perceived locus of causality rather than feeling that their actions are controlled by powers beyond them. In classrooms where teaching and learning have the purpose of autonomy development for pupils, pupils' own reflections on and talk about their own learning processes (metalearning conversations) reinforce and accelerate those very processes (Watkins, 2015).

Talking (or open-ended writing) is a key vehicle for participating in metalearning, often elicited through prompts in learning journals or metalearning journals, where learners talk or write about those factors that have helped or hindered their learning and how their awareness of this will feed into their own future learning. Chris Watkins has stressed that metalearning will only help learners self-direct their learning if the language used is owned by the learners themselves (2015, p.325). Again, the futility is highlighted of trying to *prescribe* or *impose* autonomous behaviour without the learner's considered choice. When a teacher simply provides learners with a range of study skills or strategies, the impact on learning is greatly reduced because the skills and strategies are not generated out of the learner's own reflections and volition. (See Figure 3.1 for an overview of the metalearning cycle.)

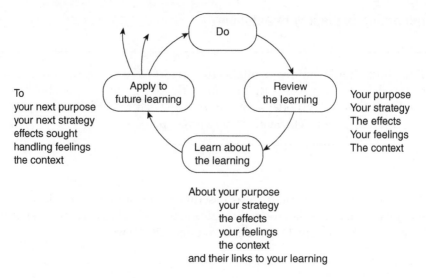

Figure 3.1   The metalearning cycle of active learning (Watkins et al., 2007, p.129)

Learners who embody a 'learning orientation' (or 'growth mindset' in Dweck's (2006) words) are likely to engage in metalearning as a matter of course, because they:

- believe that effort, including reflection and practice, can lead to success;
- believe in their ability to improve and learn, and not be fixed or stuck and not determined by being put in a particular so-called 'ability' group;
- prefer challenging tasks, whose outcome proves to them that effort, reflection and practice can lead to success;
- get satisfaction from personally defined success at difficult tasks; and
- talk to themselves: when engaged in a task, they talk themselves through it. (Based on Watkins, 2016)

Metalearning is another hugely misunderstood term which is sometimes confused with metacognition. The main difference between metalearning and metacognition is that metalearning means learning about learning while metacognition means thinking about thinking. That is, meta*learning* focuses *beyond* cognition: it includes the learner's reflection and reaction in relation to cognition, affect, motivation and elements of the social and physical context. Metacognition could be seen as a subset of metalearning.

Here are some citations from Chris Watkins' work that highlight other aspects of metalearning:

- The processing of one's experience of learning to create knowledge (2005, p.76).
- Knowing yourself as a learner – which is a good thing (Pupil cited in Watkins, 2016).
- Viewing our activity from a stance other than being solely involved in it (2015, p.322).
- Noticing what you are doing, while you are doing it (2015, p.325).

Children's words: making use of metalearning to combat fear

One distinguishing feature of metalearning, therefore, is that it is used by learners to reflect on, manage and plan for the *affective, social and physical aspects of learning* as well as the cognitive aspects. Below are some examples of year 3 and year 6 pupils' metalearning strategies for dealing with their experiences of fear in the classroom. These responses were gathered during a case study in Meadowbank Primary School, carried out during 2013, which entailed observations of classes, interviews with pupils and pupils' written sentence-completions. My findings suggested that the children's theory was that *fear was the enemy of autonomy* and they therefore sought strategies to improve their sense of autonomy as an antidote to fear. They described plenty of occasions on which they felt fear in the classroom. That was why they needed sophisticated strategies for trying to deal with this. These strategies they came up with on their own, but in interview they were able to reflect on them and discuss them in detail. Their teachers had already helped them to nurture the habit of constant reflection.

The following quotations therefore illustrated the ingenious suggestions the children came up with in how to improve learning by minimising fear and thereby increasing a sense of autonomy. They provided a clear illustration of the competent use of a metalearning approach which was part and parcel of the children's developing autonomy. They identified two distinct areas for attention: managing the physical environment including the things and other people in it; and dealing directly with their own feelings.

Children's strategies for managing the physical environment

In order to feel more autonomous and less dependent on the teacher (or others), pupils stressed the importance of being organised and having the appropriate resources ready. From among 60 children taken from both classes in the study, years 3 and 6, the following resources were described as useful for feeling autonomous:

- books
- the 'stuck board' (which explicitly had suggestions for people who were 'stuck')
- dictionaries
- thesauruses
- clear learning objectives
- self-assessments
- displays
- films
- computers
- the VCOP pyramid in which reminders about grammar and writing presentation were provided.

The children also spoke of how familiarity with their context and the people in it was a key support in diminishing their fears and increasing their sense of autonomy. In this particular school, children were strongly encouraged to collaborate and talk with peers as an everyday part of learning. Many pupils therefore unsurprisingly described their partner or friend, more often than the teacher, as one of the factors that most helped them overcome their fears. In interview, Laura and Sapphire (both year 6) mentioned that the 'phone a friend' strategy was reassuring if someone felt fearful because they lacked confidence. This strategy allowed them to choose their own source of support from among the other pupils in the class.

The pupils showed subtle insight into the kind of support a teacher should give children in order to reduce pupils' fear and increase their autonomy. Several year 6 children believed that teacher praise helped boost their autonomy and reduce their fear because it helped them realise that they could be competent. Laura (year 6) explained in interview why she thought that praise was important to dispel pupils' sense of uncertainty and dependence:

> Just to help them feel good about themselves ... Just to build up their confidence and make them happy ... Not every single lesson, because they might get a bit bored of it, but just say: 'Well done, you've improved'.

The children suggested that, more generally, evidence of their success and progress might be helpful to reinforce the child's sense of competence. In addition, they believed that a teacher who could help reduce fear and increase children's sense of autonomy was the teacher who could listen to children well and not assume that all children think and feel the same. For example, Peter and Jack (year 6) said that they felt that the autonomy-supportive teacher 'really understands you' and 'really takes the time to not just get to know you but she really helps individuals.' Delida (year 6) noted that the class teacher always let her have 'her say'. Paul (year 6) and Adelaide (year 3) particularly appreciated being able to ask the teacher questions when and where they cropped up rather than having to wait for written feedback. Sapphire drew a helpful picture of the autonomy-supporting teachers walking around among the pupils in class. Overall, they promoted the idea of the interactive classroom, rather than the silent one, so that they could work out their fears and confusions through talking with the teacher and other pupils. This way, they did not need to repress their fears but could rather take control over them.

Children's strategies for dealing with negative feelings

These meta-aware children in both classes also had conscious strategies for addressing various fears in themselves without interaction with the teacher. There were four separate sets of strategies:

- physical solutions;
- thinking about something else;
- talking with a peer; and
- making an effort directly to break through the fear.

Physical solutions

The children had worked out, through their metalearning reflections, the following physical remedies to feeling fear:

- letting off steam outside;
- playing football;
- enjoying bright colours;
- listening to calming music;
- taking a deep breath;
- drawing the scary object and throwing the drawing into the bin;
- taking it easy;
- taking as much time as needed; and
- having a break from work for a few minutes to calm down.

During my eight classroom observations in their school, I saw both teachers allowing the pupils to engage in these activities when the pupils identified it as necessary.

Thinking about something else
Ellie, in year 6, suggested one strategy for overcoming fear as distracting oneself by thinking about something different and nice:

> Talking about happier things, like, something that's happened that you're really happy about ... Like, if you go on a day out and have loads of fun.

This strategy helped children forget their fear, either temporarily or permanently. Pupils implied that it sometimes took conscious mental effort to push the fear away. For example, they explained: 'I sometimes *try and ignore* everything'; '*Block it out* so you can concentrate'; '*Pretend* it didn't happen'.

Talking
Many of the children told me that they found the best way to deal with fear was to talk with a friend. They explained that your friend might cheer you up, laugh with you or might offer to sort things out with you. One insightful child told me:

> Tell someone! If you keep it to yourself, the fear will be much greater than before.

Making an effort directly to break through the fear
Some children referred to a particular frame of mind in which, through metalearning reflection, a child could recognise their fear, work hard with it, and little by little break through to an achievement that had previously seemed too difficult. This occurred sometimes, but not always, through collaboration with a colleague. One year 3 child advised, bravely:

> Say in your head, 'Don't be scared! You can fight through the fear and enjoy the time you're with whoever-it-is-making-you-scared!'

Laura (year 6) described how she consciously taught herself to believe that the most important thing was to be having a go:

> ❛ It doesn't matter if you get it wrong or right. It's not the end of the world. It's just that you're doing your best. ❜

Several year 6 pupils indicated that this 'positive attitude' was one of the most useful strategies for learning successfully. Jack (year 6) even saw the value in being pushed beyond his comfort zone in order to grow:

> ❛ Because if you're challenged you can, you know – it makes you a better learner. You don't want to be just doing things that you just like doing ... You don't want to just be in your comfort zone ... You want to be pushed, yeah. ❜

While such moves might themselves appear frightening in some ways too, this is a fear chosen and directed by the pupil rather than the teacher. This transforms the fear into something that might ultimately help learning.

Relatedness to peers and teacher and the link to autonomy

Autonomy and collaboration with others are partners rather than rivals, as described above. Dewey suggested that autonomy hinged on the development of one's sense of identity in a social setting. An effective way for children to develop identity is through *inter-relating with* others in the classroom, both other pupils and other adults. As Dewey (1899) suggested:

> Little children have their observations and thoughts mainly directed towards people ... Their interest is of a personal rather than of an objective or intellectual sort. Its intellectual counterpart is the story-form; not the task, consciously defined end, or problem ... The study of natural objects, processes, and relations is placed in a human setting. (p.52)

Dewey suggested that the child's identity as an individual and as a member of society was nurtured by relatedness within the classroom through communication. He called for 'a spirit of free communication, of interchange of ideas, suggestions, results, both successes and failures.' He proposed at the same time to be saturating the pupil in the classroom with the 'spirit of service'. This way, 'We shall have the deepest and best guarantee of a larger society which is worthy, lovely and harmonious.' He believed that this worthy, lovely and harmonious society was supported when children used language instinctively and creatively in the classroom, through which 'We give our experiences to others and get theirs again in return'.

Ryan and Deci also linked the idea of communication to a sense of belongingness or community in the classroom. They made an essential link among competence, autonomy and *relatedness to the group and to the teacher*, as follows:

> The groundwork for facilitating internalisation [i.e. a sense of autonomy in learning] is providing a sense of belongingness and connectedness to the persons, group, or culture disseminating a goal, or what in SDT [self-determination theory] we call a sense of *relatedness*. In classrooms this means that students feeling *respected and cared for* by the teacher is essential for their willingness to accept the proffered classroom values. (Ryan and Deci, 2000, p.64)

In this sense, autonomy development, classroom talk and learning are interdependent. As noted before, a pupil's autonomy depends on being free to express themselves. It also depends on them willingly signing up to the teacher's values. This might explain why, as the Children's words below illustrate, orchestrating freely-given talk in the classroom may not be easy even when a teacher wishes to introduce it, within the confines of the traditional organisation of the classroom. In particular, children talking in front of the whole class might be frightening without that foundation of relatedness and a sense of self among others. The traditional organisation of the classroom was not designed for relatedness but explicitly for isolation in which individual judgements could be made.

Children's words: how relatedness supported autonomy

In the research described above, carried out among year 3 and year 6 pupils in Meadowbank Primary School, UK, one year 6 boy told me during an interview that as children became older, pupils became more easily inhibited by their peers, especially peers of the opposite sex in the context of the traditional classroom. Jem explained:

> If you're in year four, five and six [ages 8–11], maybe, you might get scared because you're really self-conscious kind of thing. Because you think everyone's looking at yourself ... I think I feel a bit more scared in front of the girls, because they always like giggle to each other and stuff.

Even though this particular school strongly encouraged talk among pupils, Norbert (year 6) also admitted that he was afraid to speak out in class, in case colleagues came to know him as the person who couldn't speak well in class. Andrew (year 6) said that he did not *ask* questions in class in case the other children thought he was 'weak'. On the other hand, Peter (year 6) was afraid to *answer* questions in class in case he was perceived as 'geeky'. Other year 6 pupils said they were afraid of being bullied more generally in the classroom and/or the playground and afraid of painful comments from peers, including racist comments and comments about height. I was told that sometimes a bad experience on the playground at break-time could make pupils scared during lessons, as they sat there trembling in terror of impending trouble. Jem and Paul (year 6) said they needed to feel sure that everyone was their friend before they could start to settle down to work in class; however, this was not always possible. The subsequent sense of a lack of relatedness made learning more difficult within the confines of the traditional classroom where individual judgement was still highly valued.

Among year 3 pupils, Harold reckoned that it took him 'about three days' to recover from his embarrassment when he had said something wrong in class. He had perceived that: 'Everyone started laughing and I got really embarrassed and red.' During observation, I watched another year 3 pupil, Saul, being called to the front of class to read a list off a flipchart. He was 'shivering' with fear, as he described it.

It seemed therefore that these children's classroom harboured a social atmosphere of judgement that was not sufficiently challenged to allow improved relatedness, and thereby improved autonomy. For some children, this meant that talking in front of peers could be an embarrassing situation which was worth avoiding at all costs, regardless of the destructive effects on other aspects of learning. I think that the physical layout of their classroom did not facilitate supportive relationships with peers in this school because pupils could not all see each other's faces. Besides, there were 30 children in each class. Nor did the tightly-packed curriculum help, that the teacher had to rush through. These sometimes seemed to support a more authoritarian approach, leading ultimately to the isolation and the fears described.

Given the fear they described when conversing in front of peers, I was interested to know how well peer assessment worked in these children's classrooms. Peer assessments are a good test of genuinely trusting relationships and children's sense of their own autonomy. However, the following year 3 dialogue between Saul and Anna suggested that fear lingered within the peer assessments, compromising their intended aim of nurturing autonomy:

> **EH:** Do you ever get anxious when someone's assessing your story?
>
> **Saul:** I feel a bit anxious, because I don't know what they're going to write. And if they write something – that makes me anxious just in case they write something –
>
> **EH:** Something negative? Something bad? ... And what would happen if they did? ...
>
> **Anna:** Saul would probably go cuckoo [*Laughter*] ...
>
> **Saul:** I'd feel a bit angry with them, because it's not really a kind comment.
>
> **Anna:** I just wouldn't feel confident. I wouldn't be confident in writing a story again.

In fact, all the year 3 children I interviewed told me that they worried about what their peers would say about their work during peer assessments. This again suggested that there was a social atmosphere of judgement in their classroom that had perhaps not been challenged which therefore inhibited their freedom of expression, leading to inhibited autonomy. This atmosphere was made more difficult by other worries and anxieties pupils experienced as they tried to carry out the procedures of peer assessment with limited competence: some children worried about feeding back on someone else's work, because they were not clear what they were supposed to write. Harris sometimes found his peer's work all correct so he fretted that he had nothing 'wrong' to comment on. Harold became anxious when he did not understand the assessment prompts given to him by his teacher. And Rory became stressed when he could not read his partner's writing, nor relate the assessment prompts to his own writing. As suggested vividly in Barbara Crossouard's (2011) research in Scottish primary classrooms, peer assessment that is supposed to foster autonomy – where relatedness is strong – may end up generating fear and loathing instead when the sense of competence, autonomy and/or relatedness are not fully flourishing.

Children's words: how collaborative group learning supported autonomy more effectively than the traditional classroom

It was with some of these issues in mind that teacher-researcher Rob Gratton decided to study how collaborative groups could work more successfully. He held the belief that ultimately collaborative learning was the best alternative for encouraging learners' autonomy, compared to traditional authoritarian classrooms. He noted, however, that 'What was not being offered in the literature was the clear means of how to move from general theory and context specific examples, to my own classroom practice. This led me to pursue more specifically a theory of and the principles and practices of collaborative learning' (Personal correspondence, June 2016). Below are the main findings of his initial MA dissertation study into this, which later led to the shaping of a school-wide programme in a large London state secondary school. While primary schools often group pupils in clusters of desks or tables, these groups are usually designed to keep behaviour under control and/or to keep children with similar attainment together. Primary children are rarely grouped with the intention specifically of enhancing autonomous and collaborative learning. In secondary schools, grouping pupils in the classroom at all seems to be a rarity.

However, Rob Gratton's collaborative group learning (CGL) approach is currently applied across all subjects for all students aged 11 to 16 years in the secondary school where Rob now works. Traditional, teacher dominated classrooms have become a thing of the past in this secondary school. Rob Gratton commented that over the four years he has implemented the approach, the approach had 'enhanced learner autonomy, visibly imbuing students with a capacity for lifelong-lifewide learning' (Personal correspondence, June 2016; see also www. collaborativegrouplearning.com).

In the original MA research, Gratton (2012) started by asking some students in his class about the benefits they perceived in collaborative learning and the following are some of their replies in which a hint of the groups' potential for encouraging autonomy is evident:

> Collaborative learning is when you can achieve something with some help from your group and then work independently with what you've learnt.
>
> Collaborative learning is when we have a group who helps each other instead of a teacher.
>
> Collaborative learning allows us to work as a group to greaten our chances of success through the opinions of the entire group, as opposed to one person's view.

During his history lessons, Gratton developed CGL based on three requisites:

- a diverse and stable small-group composition;
- shared knowledge-construction; and
- learner *inter*dependence.

He emphasised:

> A heterogeneous group of diverse experience, talent, and ability, is needed to enable zonal overlap (Vygotsky, 1962) enabling a process *where every learner is a novice and expert in different contexts and every learner has an opportunity to teach and be taught.* Such an interaction was perceived to be central to the optimization of the effects on learning of engaging in CGL. (Gratton, 2012; emphasis added)

Figure 3.2   CGL learning set, drawn by year 5 pupil (Hargreaves et al., 2016)

These 'diverse and stable small-groups' embodied several features likely to support autonomous learning. In particular, each person was expected to contribute their unique offering to the group and each person was respected as maturely responsible enough to act as teacher some of the time. On the other hand, interaction and collaboration were essential and constant while allowing maximum opportunities for inquiry-based tasks, initiative-taking, risk-taking and making mistakes but with relatedness to the group and the sense of belongingness there as a continuing back-up.

Gratton used a range of research methods over six months to investigate how his pupils experienced CGL in his history classroom (see Figure 3.2). By the end of that time, 28 out of 30 students felt they had benefitted from learning collaboratively in developing skills in communication and interaction – a first step in progress towards autonomy. These are some of his pupils' responses:

> I learnt to share my opinions ... and to listen.
>
> [It] made me think and share ideas.
>
> [In] listening skills, talking skills ... I am more confident.

The pupils also described developing an ability to learn with others:

> I have developed new skills like helping others.
>
> I learnt how [to] understand others and how to help them if they have problems.

Gratton noted that they perceived that they also improved their competence in academic skills. The following are some more pupil comments:

> [It] hugely improved my essay writing.
>
> I have learnt many skills that will help me in not just history but other subjects such as English.

Specifically relating to the exercise of autonomy, they perceived that they learnt skills and attributes which can be associated with a self-directed learning capacity:

> I became more independent and less afraid to discuss.
>
> If I didn't know the answer [in the past] I would just give up and not hand in work but now I don't give up and [now I] try my best.

Twenty-eight students of the 30 identified that they perceived they had increased in their learning autonomy, in some of the following ways:

> I began brainstorming ideas for myself.
>
> We had to gather our own information; this made me have to be intuitive and resourceful.

> I don't have to rely on the teacher all the time.
>
> [I] research something now using a computer.
>
> [I] stay on track and help others who are out of track and ask the teacher to help if help is really needed.

Gratton concluded that CGL seemed to have helped generate a shift away from dependence upon the teacher towards *inter*dependence within the group, in turn generating learner autonomy. Due to the group construct, multiple zones of proximal development (as described by Vygotsky) converged, enabling learners to benefit from intellectual scaffolding, appropriating skills and attributes that helped them not only to learn from each other but also to depend less on the teacher. Requests for guidance or clarification from the teacher fluctuated throughout the study but overall, gradually diminished. Even among students themselves, it seemed that they began to work with each other *inter*dependently rather than dependently, in particular sharing knowledge derived from solo research. For example, one student commented:

> Everyone had different research so everyone learnt something new or gained more information about each point.

Increased relatedness was displayed through observational evidence and more powerfully through learners' perceptions of the skills they felt they developed through CGL. In interview, they gave some extraordinarily insightful comments. For example, one pupil told Gratton:

> I learned that people that don't talk a lot have the best ideas or really good ideas to help you.

Others shared the following insights:

> [It's helpful to] take a role and use it effectively to help the group.
>
> [I improved in] working together with people that I thought I couldn't work with.
>
> [Now I] take into account – and admit – that I could be wrong sometimes.
>
> I learnt that I should be more open to helping those around me.
>
> [It was better] not jumping to conclusions.
>
> [We learnt to] give structured and constructive criticism.

These quite amazing findings illustrated how pupils learning within 'a heterogeneous group of diverse experience, talent, and ability' allowed the collaborative group to generate autonomous and collaborative learning. So long as teachers are aware of and committed to the idea of diversity rather than similarity among members of the group, this approach is emerging as one practical solution to some of the problems around encouraging autonomy through collaborative learning. It is an approach that any school can choose instead of the traditional classroom format.

Children's words: children making choices in the classroom increased their autonomous engagement

As suggested above, pupils having choice can be seen as an essential ingredient for their proactive engagement and self-direction in learning as well as for pupils making critical inquiries and comment. The provision of choice is likely to allow students to choose tasks that they perceive as consistent with their goals and interests. The opportunity to work on tasks that allow students to realise their goals or meet their interests contributes to students' experience of first, engagement and second, autonomy in learning. 'Fostering relevance' has been identified as one of the most important predictors of engagement in school work (Katz and Assor, 2007) and is greatly enhanced when students have choice. It appears that this is likely to be particularly important in the case of academic school activities because academic activities are not always (very rarely?) intrinsically motivated. This means that it is more difficult to encourage pupils to 'buy-in' to the teacher's agenda. Choice may be one answer to this difficulty. However, in order to introduce choice into a classroom where it is unfamiliar, some initiation and practice will be required to start off with. Good choices and decisions will be made in collaboration with the teacher at first, who acts as 'a mature, responsible decision maker who deliberately models decision making for students and coaches them in the skills of making good choices' (Starnes and Paris, 2000, p.395).

Christine Yeomans, teacher-researcher and then-MA student, explored directly students' experiences of choice in the UK classroom in order to understand and operationalise choice better in her own secondary history classroom (Yeomans, 2013). Her field research was guided by three questions:

1. Do students favour the provision of choices in their learning?
2. What types of choices do students welcome?
3. Under what specific circumstances do they say that choice is effective for learning?

Yeomans had already concluded the following from surveying the limited existing research about choice in classrooms (e.g. Katz and Assor, 2007; Patall et al., 2008; Assor, 2012; Patall, 2012):

- Students must believe they have a genuine choice and are truly free to select the option they want. That is, they must sense that their autonomy or volition is genuine.
- The two or more choices offered should be of equivalent value and there should be no pressure to select a particular option. Again, volition is essential here.

- By itself, having a choice does not necessarily lead to increased motivation, but this effect is more likely if the outcome is considered meaningful or valuable. Offering choices that allow a degree of personalisation and include a range of learning strategies are some possible ways of making learning more personally relevant.
- Choice has the greatest effect on engagement and autonomy when students are presented with between three and five options.
- When choosing becomes overwhelming, exhausting or difficult (for whatever reason), engagement may decline. This finding underlines the physical and emotional aspects of learning and their impact on exercising autonomy.
- Choices with critical consequences may inhibit performance. For example, choices that place a student under public scrutiny, focus on the demonstration of performance or involve comparisons with peers may produce high levels of anxiety and lead to choice avoidance or other ego-protecting strategies. Once again, the normalising judgement appears to be the enemy of free choice selection.

Yeomans was lucky enough to be welcomed into the classrooms of colleagues who had incorporated choice regularly into their lessons. She carried out observations and interviews in these classrooms.

Students welcomed choice

Students seemed to welcome having a balance between teacher-led activities and those that entailed student choice and collaborative group work. For example, Tom (year 9) expressed that it was:

❝ Nice to have a balance, sometimes choose, sometimes good to be directed. ❞

Choices were recognised and appreciated by the students for a wide variety of reasons, including the following three.

1. Choices could make lessons more engaging

Students often mentioned that having choices could make lessons more engaging by adding variety as well as encouraging creativity and different ways of thinking. Initiative-taking and self-direction were therefore encouraged where choice was available. For example:

❝ It makes us more creative ... encourages you to think for yourself. (Steve, year 7)

You have to think more about how you're going to go about it, and then sometimes it can make you – it can get you to think in different areas of what you are doing and then you learn more. (Debbie, year 7) ❞

Some students, such as Philip (year 10), emphasised the importance of choice in terms of relatedness, by explaining how important it was to choose whether to work alone or in groups, and to choose who to work with:

> Choosing who to work with helps learning. When teachers choose groups it's harder because you don't always feel comfortable sharing ideas. (Carol, year 9)

Mark (year 9) appreciated being able to choose where to sit, but in his case he often preferred the back where people were not looking over his shoulder 'checking what you are doing'. He said that this judgemental process made him feel confined because he felt that 'everything has to be correct' and this was counterproductive to his proactive engagement and self-direction.

Students also thought that choice provision improved their relationship with their teacher, for example:

> It gives you more trust with your teacher. (Philip, year 10)
>
> This makes a friendlier working relationship. (Sarah, year 10)

2. Choices helped to tailor learning to individual preferences

This was one of the most frequent reasons given by students, because in this case, choice enhanced their sense of self. For example, when you have choice:

> It's easier to find out what you like and what works best for you. (Sarah, year 10)
>
> You are learning in a way that is better for you and learning more. (Tom, year 9)

Participants also mentioned that choices helped them to adjust the level of challenge of an activity to suit themselves, for example:

> If you are finding it a bit easy you can take it up to your own level because you've got the freedom. (Debbie, year 7)

Students reported enjoying having options about how to *present* their work, for example by film, computer presentation or poster. This was because:

> It allows people who learn in different ways to choose what works for them best. And that's good. (Sarah, year 10)
>
> I really like having choices. It's really good because if you really are bad at iPads, it's good that you can do it on paper. If you got told that you had to use the iPad then it wouldn't be that good. (Melanie, year 7)

3. Choices facilitated a feeling of well-being because of each pupil taking more mature responsibility for learning

The majority of the students, regardless of their age or gender, reported positive emotions and an enhanced sense of mature responsibility as a result of being provided with choices in the classroom.

First, they reported feeling happier, more comfortable and relaxed when they were allowed some freedom. They savoured the additional sense of well-being that having choice generated in them. As Steve (year 7) admitted:

> I don't really like being told what to do by the teacher.

And Anita (year 9) agreed:

> [Choice] makes you feel like you have more freedom ... it makes you feel better than if you are just told to do something.

In addition to experiencing more freedom from restriction, students also reported feeling more appreciated because they saw the provision of choice as an expression of trust towards them and felt a heightened sense of their own authority. For example:

> I feel like, like you're given your own sense of responsibility, 'cause they're trusting you to make a good choice. It makes you feel more responsible and it makes you feel happier that you are trusted to make your own choice. (Sophie, year 7)
>
> It makes you feel like you are in charge and more responsible for what you do ... you become more enthusiastic about what you do. (Tom, year 9)

These feelings were particularly strong for year 10 students, for example:

> I'm growing up so I want a bit more responsibility. It's nice to have the freedom to choose what you want to have. (Philip, year 10)
>
> It makes you feel more grown up, kind of trusted, like a person, not just a student, telling you what to do and stuff like that. (Sarah, year 10)

Negative aspects of having choice

Although students generally liked having choices and thought that these could make a positive contribution to their autonomous learning, they were also aware of the circumstances in which choice was most effective. In particular they found choice counter-productive when too many alternatives were presented; when making the 'right' choice was a source of anxiety (as with GCSE choices); when it had negative social repercussions; and when it didn't fit in with their mood or motivational state at that time, for example when they were too tired to make the effort.

Students of all ages were clear about what might help them to make good choices and offered some specific suggestions for classroom practice. In this context, the most frequently mentioned issue was having sufficient competence to be confident of their choice. This competence could be, for example, background knowledge, skills or an understanding of the assessment criteria. In other words, students expressed a need to feel confident about their learning before facing choices. For example, Debbie in year 7 said:

> If I don't know what we are doing particularly, haven't ever gone into that area before, I prefer to be taught a bit more about it sometimes.

Tom in year 9 commented:

> If you are really struggling with an aspect it is probably easier for someone to tell you what to do. You are already not feeling very confident about it and then have a choice placed on you: you could end up not doing much. So if you are really struggling it would be better to have some guidance.

Along similar lines, students recognised and welcomed guidance and structure that supported the process of making a choice and made it more manageable. For example, with reference to one class that Yeomans observed, Steve (year 7) commented that:

> We usually get offered a lot more choices but today as it was such a big task he was helping us by narrowing it down.

He added that he found it helpful when:

> Teachers give us a briefing, tell us about the choices, make us feel comfortable, talk more about the task. Because sometimes they don't go into much depth at the start.

Although students liked to have the flexibility of choosing to work with others, they recognised that this option was not without its problems, and this was especially noted by year 9 students. In that group Carol mentioned that she sometimes felt anxious about the group selecting process, worrying that she might get left out. And Anita explained how, in the lesson that Yeomans had observed, she had wanted to work alone but had found it hard to say 'no' to a friend who wanted to work with her: and who she knew was considerably less motivated by her studies than she was. None the less, all students were adamant that they would still prefer to have the option to choose their learning companions despite these issues. For these students, 'power over what is taught and learned, how it is taught and learned, where it is taught and learned, when it is taught and learned and what the general learning environment is like' were indeed partly in the *hands of pupils* (Meighan and Harber, 2007, p.238).

Children's words: pupils experienced that autonomously choosing talk-partners supported their engagement, enjoyment and metalearning capacity

Building on the notion that choice is an important aspect of autonomous learning and also that children care most about *people*, another teacher-researcher and then-MA student engaged in a research project which explored children's choice of talk-partner (Filer, 2014). John Filer taught a year 5 class in a London primary school who were deemed by the other year 5 teachers in the school as difficult to teach. Jon Filer's job was therefore to manage this 'difficult' class and bring their attainment scores up to the level of the other two classes of year 5 children. His targets for achievement were that 73 per cent of his class would attain at 3B or above, which for most children would be three sub-levels of 'progress' in half a year. Two sub-levels of 'progress' in one year was normally considered challenging by most teachers in primary schools in England. This was therefore a tall order and one on which Filer's salary also depended! Rather than being fearful and doing more of the same activities that his class were used to, Filer decided to take a risk and try some new strategies to engage his class and increase their autonomy for learning.

His classroom was normally set out in five groups of six pupils who had been positioned so that they were, in his (teacher's) view, most likely to learn well. For example, he put girls and boys in each group so that the boys did not become too noisy or distracted.

One day, however, he invited the individuals in one group of children instead to choose whom they sat with that day. Each child in that group went to sit with whichever talk-partner they themselves believed they would work with best. The displaced children filled their empty spaces in a new group of six. At the end of that day, Filer met with the six children who had chosen their talk-partners and discussed with them how the change had affected their learning that day.

The next day, the first group returned to their original places. Then Filer offered a different group of children the choice to sit with talk-partners they believed would be most conducive to their learning. Again, he later discussed with them how they had experienced their learning during that day.

Each day over five days, Filer gave this choice to a different group of children. In the second week, he began the process over again. But this time he reminded the children to reflect back on their experience of choosing a talk-partner last week. Some children therefore chose different partners on this second occasion of choice. Some chose the same.

In the third week, Filer did the process one last time for the final five days of the research project. Then he had a lengthy whole-class conversation about the children's reflections on the process. There were two rather extraordinary outcomes. First, all the children wanted to continue with this process ad infinitum. No one wanted to return to prescribed groupings because the new system suited their learning so much better. For example, pupil Eva suggested that you 'don't get bored of the same person'; and Arjun added that 'you can change if you don't get on with a person'. Calypso noted that by sitting next to different friends she would be exposed to different opinions that would help with her learning, rather than being 'stuck with one person'. Hattie, a child who had only been at the school for two months, saw the choice as a way to meet and get to know more members of the class. Eva was happy because she finally managed to sit on a table of all girls. She found this helpful because, as her friend pointed out, boys 'fight and then cry and not get on with their work ... and then I can't get on with mine'. The children who had been placed on the 'low' attainers' table liked being able to move because of the stigma attached to the 'low' attainers' table.

The second rather extraordinary outcome was that these 'difficult' children displayed an exceptionally insightful view of the kind of talk-partner who would support their own learning. For example, pupil Dieter pointed out that the right partner for him was someone who 'won't really bother me' so that he could 'get more done'. Pupil Lauri continued that this could be a problem with her regular partner, Archie, because he was 'silly and distracts me a lot'. Arjun and Zendaya told Filer that sitting next to Lucas, on the other hand, hindered their learning due to him being unable or unwilling to help with their work; he was referred to as 'too quiet'. Some children preferred to sit with people whom they considered as 'smarter' than they were, but, as Filer pointed out, their criteria for deciding who was 'smart' did not tally with his own. Filer suggested that someone a child believed to be 'smart' was actually someone in whom they had confidence.

In general, having fun and being happy were seen by all the groups as an important attribute to sitting with the right person. However, pupil Hattie acknowledged that there was a fine line between a happy 'chat' and a distraction: 'If you are next to someone who is talking and you can't concentrate then that is not good'. Sitting next to one's friend could be seen as part of choosing the right person to sit next to. As Helen noted, her friend Bevan was a good friend who would never get her in trouble and would 'tell her to stop if she is being naughty'. Ewan elaborated that friends work well together and 'won't argue' and you 'enjoy your learning more' because of it. Eduardo explained the problem with sitting next to someone who was not your friend:

> If you are sitting next to someone you are not really friends with you will be grumpy all the time. You won't get much work done, 'cause if you are doing partner work and you don't get on with them it will affect your learning.

Children chose at the start of the research to sit next to friends. However, over the course of time, thinking changed, as Zendaya reflected:

> Before, I was just thinking who was my friend. Now I think I will sit next to someone who will be really helping me, like Helena or Eva.

Genesis concurred, explaining:

> I will choose a sensible person as well. I will not just choose a friend as I get distracted and I talk too much.

This may have been said to please the teacher, but during the research this was a theme that was being reflectively discussed by quite a few of the children.

Filer was brave enough to continue allowing student choice of talk-partners after the end of the research. He noticed a shift in the pupils' approach to learning from disengaged to more engaged, from dependent to more proactively self-directed. They were all more skilled in making critical inquiries. Lauri, for example, told him that she had now taken control:

> I felt in control as I got to choose who I was going to sit next to. Usually I don't get to choose.

Amazingly, Filer also got nearer to reaching his prescribed targets with this class and did not undergo a drop in salary. It seemed that during this research, his focus on pupils' competence, autonomy *and* relatedness led to enhanced learning.

ACTIVITIES FOR CLASSROOM PRACTICE: SOME PRACTICAL WAYS FORWARD FOR TEACHERS AND OTHER EDUCATORS IN CLASSROOMS

Discussion or journal writing

Discuss or note down the ideas that Chapter 3 has suggested for helping learners feel more in the driving seat. Using the sections above, consider the following:

- Learners developing ways for handling negative feelings in the classroom.

- Learners confronting the social atmosphere of judgement.

- Learners engaging in collaborative group learning.

- Learners choosing who they learn with.

- Learners choosing what they do.

- Learners choosing environmental resources for learning.

Actions to try out

Try asking pupils to make choices, especially in relation to assessing how and with whom they learn most fruitfully (which may not be the same as quietly!).

What happens when the teacher discusses choice with students explicitly on a regular basis, as one aspect of encouraging learning?

Keep a tally over one lesson of how often learners have *genuine* choice or the chance to express a sense of *self* through taking initiatives.

Plenary

Describe, reflect on and analyse for yourself or in a pair/group, what happened when these actions were tried out in classrooms.

How will you engage pupils in evaluating any of the ideas you try out?

Finally, note down how 'autonomous' you feel as a teacher/educator.

Where would you like more autonomy in your teaching and how would that help you and help students?

4

Teacher feedback in the classroom

> ❝ [The teacher's feedback] made me not listen and it was really annoying! I can do this, but you keep repeating it, actually distracting me instead of – because I was told to think, and then – (Laila, year 5) ❞

Chapter 4 investigates pupils' responses to teachers' classroom feedback, with a special emphasis on whether or how the teacher's feedback seemed to support their autonomous learning. This chapter draws extensively on my research project in a year 5 classroom in Emerald Primary School, Surrey, UK, over six months in 2012, whereby a group of pupils reported regularly on how they found the classroom and how they interpreted the teacher's comments (also referred to in Chapter 3). The work of Harry Torrance and John Pryor (1998) is used as a framework for theorising feedback.

The traditional definition of 'feedback'

I happened to come across the following feedback sequence in the mathematics exercise book of Indigo, a year 3 pupil (aged 7), as provided by his teacher over a couple of weeks' maths lessons. Given its judgemental and negative tone, it is easy to imagine how Indigo, who received the feedback, felt about maths thereafter. It was particularly galling for him, given that he was dyslexic and found writing difficult. The teacher wrote:

> ❝ Please see me straight away. I am not at all happy with your work in this group.
>
> No work done today.
>
> This took 25 minutes. Did you listen when we went through these on the board?
>
> Where is your work? Did this really take 20 minutes? ❞

The word 'feedback' has also appeared in electronics. Perhaps this unlikely source helps explain the confusion surrounding the conception and use of feedback in the classroom. In electronics, feedback can be equated to a high-pitched and almost unbearable screech. Perhaps that was exactly how the pupil, Indigo, experienced it when he received the feedback above. (See also the comments of Laila, above, who found her teacher's feedback 'really annoying').

In traditional, authoritarian classrooms, feedback tends to be thought of as the teacher's judgement on the performance of a pupil. In some countries, it is simply thought of as 'knowledge of results' (KR) in the form of a mark or grade without comment. It is a judgement about whether a student has met the required standards. Teachers from Pakistan, China and Egypt that I have worked with, for example, have been surprised when definitions of feedback included teachers' explanatory comments, especially verbal ones.

In Britain, the traditional conception of feedback tends to accord with the F of the closed IRF sequence: **I**nitiation by the teacher, **R**esponse by the pupil or pupils, and **F**eedback by the teacher on how well the response met her/his expectation. In a traditional or authoritarian classroom where the teacher is overly dominant in terms of acting as the *primary knower* and the *monitor or judge* of value (Nassaji and Wells, 2000), the autonomy of the learner may be threatened by the nature of the teacher's feedback, as discussed in Chapter 3. Lin (2007), from the context of Hong Kong, described how the IRF sequence, in its traditional form, helped teachers in their role as classroom *managers* and as primary *knowers* (rather than educators) by embracing two functions: the *converging function* and the *certifying function*. The converging function of IRF helped the teacher to 'maintain tight control and minimise digression' (p.88), while the certifying function 'work[ed] students' input into acceptable answers to exam-type questions, that is, to certify it as correct and model answers' (p.88). Within this process, certifying information took priority over personal information, such as a child's thoughts, ideas or feelings, and the teacher might not trust the class to reach the required information level through pupil-led dialogue. The pace of the traditional IRF classroom tended to be fast, allowing little time for pupils or their teacher to pause and reflect, sometimes resulting in talk moving from one focus to another non-sequentially and thereby potentially losing genuine meaning.

Lin (2007) commented that both convergence and certification functioned primarily through the teacher's 'feedback', the 'F' in the IRF sequence. Thus the concept of 'feedback' that has developed within this context of the authoritarian classroom takes both a converging and certifying function, leaving little room for learners' initiatives or critical, divergent responses, quite apart from paying any attention to the relational sides of feedback and learning.

Divergent and process-focused feedback

Feedback needs to accord with purposes for schooling just as teaching does. If teaching now aims to encourage competence, autonomy and relatedness, then one could argue that feedback needs to do so too. Managing and certifying the child is not an adequate description of a teacher's role if the purpose of state schooling is either *the growth of individuals* or the development of a *critically educated citizenry able to engage reflectively and reflexively with the wider society* (Schiro, 2013; see Chapter 1).

Gipps et al. (2000) distinguished between *evaluative* feedback, which was just judgemental as in the traditional IRF sequence, and *descriptive* feedback, which explained why something was good or not. In 1998, Harry Torrance and John Pryor in their work *Investigating Formative Assessment*, developed an assessment framework which took the categories in a different direction, distinguishing between *convergent* and *divergent* assessment, moving away from the traditional definitions of feedback within the IRF sequence. Assessment, and therefore also feedback, would be 'convergent' when its purpose was to 'remediate' on a route towards a particular (prescribed) learner competence, but would be 'divergent' when its aim was to encourage further learner inquiry on a route towards learner autonomy. Within a 'divergent' assessment framework, John Pryor and Barbara Crossouard (2008, p.4) described feedback as 'exploratory, provisional or *provocative*'. Divergently-framed feedback would often encourage children to reconstruct their thinking about a subject *domain* or a learning *process*. Indeed, it might encourage reflection also on the wider social context of learning.

With *descriptive* feedback (Gipps et al., 2000), judgements are elaborated on using a description to guide the pupil's next actions. Black and Wiliam (2006) called this also *directive* feedback. But this feedback but did not suggest that the pupil engaged in self-directed proactive further inquiry. In terms of supporting children's learning autonomy, *provocative* feedback comments may be more useful than purely *descriptive* or *directive* feedback. For example, in a literacy task, feedback might be:

- ✓ *Descriptive:* Go away and correct these three spelling mistakes because they are incorrect.
- ✓ *Provocative:* Can you think of some clever ways to remember how to spell these three words in future? Come and show me which ways you create.

In history:

- ✓ *Descriptive:* Correct those dates. Those are not the right dates.
- ✓ *Provocative:* What else was going on at the same time? Can you find out some other important events that happened at the same time?

Coming from a slightly different angle, but still focusing on learning autonomy, John Hattie and Helen Timperley (2007) defined *process-focused/self-regulation-focused feedback* as teacher comments that supported the learner to reconsider their own learning processes and how to make these more effective. Hattie and Timperley suggested that feedback on self-regulatory processes might be most useful if they would:

- encourage the learner to reflect on their own strategies;
- refer to the competencies the learner had already gained;
- refer to the learner's *own* goals;
- never compare one learner with another; and
- emphasise the effectiveness of effort, *but only when the learner was succeeding.*

Feedback focusing on the self

Hattie and Timperley (2007) actually identified four focuses for feedback. These are presented below in reverse order of effectiveness for autonomous learning, suggesting that a focus on the child's learning processes and self-regulation would be most useful:

1. Self (not effective).
2. Task (not effective for longer-term learning).
3. Task processes (effective for transferring skills to other tasks).
4. Self-regulatory processes (effective for longer-lasting learning because it feeds into learner autonomy).

Here are some examples of teacher feedback in relation to the first focus, 'self'. Feedback on this focus might be particularly *un*helpful because it makes the recipient feel judged, drawing in distracting but very strong emotions:

- You're a clever boy, I'm very pleased with you. [The child gets distracted by thinking: 'I'm so great!']
- I'm disappointed with your work. You should do better. [The child gets distracted by thinking: 'I'm so useless!']
- This was good work. It's much better than the work of other children in your group. [The child gets distracted by thinking 'I'm so great, I'd better keep competing!']
- What would your father think of this? [The child gets distracted by feeling fear.]

Self-related feedback most often takes the form of praise or reprimand. This relates to the *evaluative* feedback of Gipps et al. (2000). This was indeed the feedback these authors found most common in their primary classroom research. It appeared that some primary teachers, especially, tried to use praise as much as they could with the aim of encouraging pupils to keep trying and to make them feel confident about themselves. While feelings of competence are essential among pupils, and play a pivotal role in their developing identities, it seems that unelaborated praise can be counter-productive (Torrance and Pryor, 1998; Henderlong and Lepper, 2002; Dweck, 2006). Such feedback not only taps into the child's distracting ego-based emotions but also provides little support for either competence or autonomy when no elaboration is provided. Ryan and Deci (2000), referring to self-determination theory, warned that feedback would only be acted upon when the learner had a sense of autonomy as well as competence when receiving feedback. What erodes the pupil's sense of both autonomy and competence in the case of unelaborated praise is that it puts the teacher into the role of *monitor* or *judge* of value (Nassaji and Wells, 2000) without providing the criteria against which her/his judgements are made. As discussed in Chapter 2, this can give the pupil a sense that the teacher has unfettered power while the child has no means of evaluating the legitimacy of the teacher's authority. The following examples taken from a range of pupil exercise books illustrate how the teacher can take the stance of judge rather than educator:

> This is excellent again. Your science work is very good.
>
> I like your story!
>
> 8/10
>
> B +
>
> Well done.
>
> Good effort.

However, detached praise like this could contribute better to autonomous learning and increased competence by adding a description, which then allows the learner to recognise (and perhaps critique) the criteria being used for the judgement.

In a survey of teachers' views about feedback (see Hargreaves, 2011), teachers said they believed that feedback would be less randomly successful and more fool-proof for autonomous learning if:

- the learner asks for it or gives their willing consent for it;
- it is about something the learner wishes to be fed back on;
- it is provided at a time when the student has time to think about it and act on it;
- it is given during an activity or task so that the student can use the feedback while it is still fresh in their mind;
- it is little and often;
- positive achievements, past and present, are stressed; and
- it encourages pupils to take action to continue or improve current progress.

While feedback about the child's 'self' appears to be distracting and to erode their sense of autonomy, feedback that takes the child's autonomy and relatedness into account, as well as their competence, seems to be what teachers believed to be most appropriate. The first three considerations given above seem to stress this: feedback is likely to engage the pupil when the learner asks for it or gives their willing consent for it; when it is about something the learner wishes to be fed back on; when it is provided at a time when the student has time to think about it and act on it. These three considerations put the child at the heart of the feedback, showing a more respectful approach to the child's particular motivations for learning and their capacity for exercising their own authority than in the traditional constructs. These three considerations in particular recognise that, in order to act on feedback, the pupil needs to judge the value in feedback in order to gain the personal motive to act. As Knud Illeris emphasised in his seminal book *How We Learn* (2007), without having a convincing incentive to start engaging, the child may not ever start to notice feedback. This will only happen if they sign up to the teacher's values and have an incentive for progressing, whether an internalised incentive or an intrinsic incentive (see Deci and Ryan, 2000). I think that this is what we as teachers sometimes forget to ask: why should the children pay attention to our feedback? What's in it for them? It is really no surprise that even the most detailed and accurate feedback given by teachers gets ignored (see Sadler, 1989). This is where conversations about purposes for learning are so important, both among teachers and pupils. This is also what led Philipe Perrenoud (1998) to write:

> Part of the feedback given to pupils in class is like *so many bottles thrown out to sea*. No one can be sure that the message they contain will one day find a receiver ... some of the messages which the teacher conceives as feedback do not in fact play this role for the pupil. (p.86)

Mary James (2006) illustrated an alternative model for feedback in which feedback was actually directed *by* pupils: she conceptualised feedback to constitute the responses emanating from an audience of other learners to authentic learning products. In this model, it was a community of learners who took the principal responsibility for constructing 'feedback' together. Sometimes this feedback might have been as simple as showing spontaneous appreciation. In this model, the 'feedback' constructed related to how well a task was received by its intended audience, including both experts and novices: the crucial point was, however, that *the intended audience had been nominated by the learner themselves*. In this way, the learner was invested in the feedback and likely to be interested to listen to what the chosen audience had to say.

What has become crystal clear from all the published research is that feedback is highly complex and involves a range of physical, social, affective, cognitive and even political factors. Its effectiveness is related to the goals of the teachers and learners under consideration. In classrooms where the culture emphasises that *'the purpose of education is to help children learn the accumulated knowledge of our culture: that of the academic disciplines'* (see Schiro's four philosophies in Chapter 1), the effectiveness of feedback may be judged in relation to how much 'knowledge' pupils have managed to retain. From this collectionist perspective, pupils' memorisation, retention and understanding might be the focus of teachers' feedback judgements. Since these outputs are seen as quantifiable rather than fluid, little comment is deemed necessary. Even so, other factors will affect whether or how pupils can carry out the tasks of memorisation, retention and understanding. Pupils will still need the incentive to start engaging with feedback, and where this is missing, teachers may turn to coercion to make pupils pay attention to their feedback.

It is this complex and multi-faceted nature of 'feedback' that the pupils' words below illustrated. They suggested that the traditional notion of feedback as the teacher's evaluative comment on the pupil might indeed need further consideration.

Children's words: what pupils said about teacher feedback

Nine year 5 pupils in Emerald Primary School, Surrey, UK, agreed to participate in an investigation of their responses to the teacher's feedback over a period of six months. I observed them during classes and then talked to them about their responses to the teacher feedback that I had seen (and had also captured on video for them to see). The teacher, known here as Mrs K, categorised four of the nine pupils as 'high' attainers, two as 'middle' attainers and three as 'low' attainers, against National Curriculum targets.

Certain pupils required more support for being autonomous

Seven of the nine children, including all the 'lower' attainers, expressed considerable frustration when their teacher continued to give feedback after it was necessary (see for example Laila's comment at the start of this chapter). They did not like the teacher to keep repeating her feedback or to spoon-feed them when they could manage by themselves. Farhana told me that she found it more helpful to have to look up a spelling rather than having it spelled out for her. She commented, 'You would remember how to spell it because you did it.' Likewise, Esther preferred the teacher to give her feedback using a question, because this provoked her to think more deeply for herself.

Laila shocked me by saying that she had worked out that the teacher gave more directive, 'spoon-feeding' feedback to 'lower' attainers:

> ❜ If you're on the 'highest' table [the teacher] sort of expects you to work it out and if you can't work it out, she expects you [to try] a bit more. Like on the lower tables, she says, 'Oh, we'll help you' and you're just stuck on the same question [as those on the 'highest' table]. But then she tries to give you the answer! ... I want to work it out by myself. I want her to explain the example one so we all have examples – it's just ... I really want to know how to do it! ❜

This quote illustrated Laila's experience of having self-direction discouraged in the classroom through the teacher's overly-directive feedback. Other studies have also illustrated teachers' more limited dialogue and negative feedback in 'lower' sets and the resulting disaffection and low self-esteem of 'lower' set students (Boaler et al., 1998; see also Chapter 5 in relation to 'ability' grouping). To check out Laila's hunch, I decided to work out the average number of autonomy versus non-autonomy promoting feedback comments the class teacher addressed to children in different attainment groups across four lessons, two in which the teacher focused on the group of 'low' attainers and two in which she focused on the group of 'high' attainers.

For this exercise, autonomy-*promotion* was coded when the teacher feedback was encouraging the pupil's:

- *singularity,* usually in the sense of the child cultivating a view that might stand out from the general view;
- *proactivity in learning,* manifested through that child's initiative-taking or unsolicited engagement with a topic; Mrs K sometimes encouraged proactivity using humour;

- *metasocial critical inquiry*, which was subdivided into: first, metasocial critical inquiry into rules about life; and second, metasocial critical inquiry into relationships, including social relationships occurring during learning; and
- *critical inquiry* into learning processes.

On the other hand, I defined *non*-autonomy promoting feedback as follows. These categories consisted of teacher feedback intending to promote the pupil's:

Continuation or cessation of a particular activity: In this case, the teacher showed approval or disapproval, e.g. Mrs K said, 'Oh! I like that' to show approval and 'Oh, grrrrr!' to indicate disapproval. This category accorded with Gipps et al.'s (2000, p.92) *evaluative* feedback category of 'expressing approval and disapproval'.

Correct answer: The teacher asked a closed question as her feedback, which was sometimes disguised as an open question, e.g. she asked the closed question during literacy, 'It's an adverb because it ends in ....?'.

Feelings of shame or pride: Mrs K evaluated the pupil *self*, e.g. she told Aaron, 'You rush through things – you're a bright lad, you're all very bright on this table ... but you mustn't rush.' This is the feedback that Hattie and Timperley (2007) suggested might be destructive to learning because involvement of the ego distracted the learner.

Certainty about correctness: The teacher confirmed that an answer was right, e.g. 'You're absolutely right'. This reassuring feedback resonated with Gipps et al.'s (2000, p.92) category of *descriptive* feedback named 'telling children they are right'.

Increased understanding: The teacher repeated or explained an answer, sometimes elaborating extensively, e.g. Mrs K repeated a pupil's answer as follows: '"Five frisky foals" ... they link together, those two words, don't they, because often, foals are described as being frisky'. On another occasion, even though Vijay had physically demonstrated a 'glimpse' convincingly, she proceeded to elaborate, 'it's not stop-and-have-a-look, is it? It's like Vijay said, you just glance at it, then you choo-choo by'. This feedback could be described as bordering on autonomy-promoting.

Grasp of the correct answer: The teacher provided or pre-empted an answer, e.g. she asked Laila why she had to put an extra piece of wood into the catapult she was building, but before Laila could answer, Mrs K intercepted, 'It was because the cam, the cam on the shelf, wasn't wide enough'.

Action: The teacher instructed a pupil to act, as her feedback, e.g. in response to Josh telling her that he got the first test question right, she instructed, 'Let's keep going'.

Over four recorded lessons, I found that the teacher, Mrs K, gave less autonomy-promoting feedback to 'lower' attaining children than to 'higher' attaining pupils.

Laila's suspicion was supported by a count of the instances of autonomy-promoting feedback among the 'lowest' attaining children. The average number of instances of such feedback was 1.8 instances per minute for the two 'high' attainers' lessons observed, compared to 0.6 instances per minute for the lessons focusing on the 'lower' attainers. That is, *the teacher made three times as many autonomy-promoting feedback comments to the 'high' attainers than to the 'low' attainers.* Of course, these might have been uncharacteristic lessons in this respect but the figures for non-autonomy promoting feedback did not show a different pattern for these lessons. The comments from the pupils themselves also supported the conclusion that Mrs K gave 'lower' attainers less autonomy-promoting feedback.

Yet, despite receiving less autonomy-promoting feedback, I saw examples of the 'lower' attainers displaying behaviour that seemed to display autonomy. For example, Dave commented that he preferred to ask for the teacher's help when he needed it, rather than receiving it all the time (see his comments at the start of Chapter 3). Such comments suggested that these children were capable of autonomous learning. Perhaps if the teacher had given them more autonomy-promoting feedback, they could have made greater progress in this area.

It may be that the teacher did not consider the pupils who attained lower levels against the National Curriculum to be as capable as their higher-attaining peers in terms of singularity, proactive engagement or critical inquiry (i.e. of autonomy). Of course, by acting on these beliefs she might also have been making them come true. In interview, Mrs K was clearly eager to provide equal opportunities to all learners. However, when asked about the idea of building up a culture in the classroom where all participants could have a frank discussion, she made a comment that suggested she thought that only some children were maturely responsible enough and others were not. She did not suggest how she would promote increased 'maturity'. She said:

> Yeah, if you developed [the culture] it would probably work. It would depend on the cohort of children, their maturity.

The numerical data relating to autonomy-promoting feedback in this study were useful in that they raised the concern that the teacher used autonomy-promoting feedback with 'low' attaining children less than with others. It raised the question of whether this applied to Mrs K in all her lessons, and also whether it applies to other teachers.

Certain children required increased direction and elaboration

Sometimes the children in Mrs K's class wanted *increased* attention and direction, especially those in the 'higher' attaining group. Mia said:

> Sometimes it's a bit annoying when you need more help, but then she doesn't – she just says, 'Work it out', and you're thinking, 'Well, how?'. But if you don't get it, how can you try? Because you don't know how to do it.

Esther, categorised by Mrs K as a 'high' attaining child, did not understand the written feedback notes that the teacher had written on Esther's literacy exercise book. At one point I asked Esther what the feedback meant but she admitted that she could not actually read it. Somewhere else, the teacher described her essay as an 'epic', but Esther did not know what the word 'epic' meant. More commonly though, she told me that she would have liked more explanation with her feedback. She seemed to require elaboration and examples rather than just direction, more descriptive and provocative feedback rather than just evaluative feedback. The following interview dialogue illuminated her problems and the reasons why she wanted more elaboration. It also highlighted the different assumptions of the teacher compared to the pupil:

> **EH:** Do ticks mean – what do they mean on this page?
>
> **Esther:** I don't actually know. She just puts a tick, so I actually don't know what it means. I think it just means 'Well done', but I think they should write a comment, because tick, to me, doesn't actually mean anything. It's just a line in your book.
>
> **EH:** Right, so you don't know what that means ... Okay, here she's put 'Excellent notes, Esther'. What did you think about when you got that?
>
> **Esther:** I thought I'd written good description, maybe, but I think she should write what's excellent about it, because putting 'Excellent notes' won't actually tell me to keep writing what I've done. Because if I know that I've done good adverbs, then I know that I need to keep doing that and keep that up, but just putting 'Excellent notes' doesn't actually help.
>
> **EH:** ... Then next page she's put a smiley face. 'Excellent detail and description included.'
>
> **Esther:** Mm. I think this bit's good, because it actually tells, 'Detail and description'. Then I know I'm good at that, and I need to keep that up. But just putting 'Excellent' doesn't actually help.

Similarly, Esther did not find it useful when the teacher simply put 'sp' against a spelling mistake in her writing, because then she still did not know how to spell the word correctly. On the other hand, Esther highlighted an example of the teacher's provocative feedback as one of the most effective pieces of feedback she had been given: the occasion when the teacher introduced her to an online thesaurus when she had asked how to spell a word. Esther had used this thesaurus repeatedly since then, both at school and at home.

Children's comments on how feelings affected their responses to feedback

In relation to Illeris' (2007) suggestion that an incentive is needed to jump-start engagement in learning, I was particularly interested in what children had to say about their own feelings and how these influenced their engagement with teacher feedback. The nine children in this study described a range of negative emotions associated with the teacher's feedback, which might be supposed to limit engagement: in addition to anger, they mentioned frustration, fear, anxiety, nervousness, embarrassment, hostility and confusion. This was despite the fact that their teacher, Mrs K, was an extremely warm, generous and friendly person as they all agreed. None the less, Laila described becoming fearful before receiving the teacher's feedback, in case she was wrong. Then Dave also suggested that the teacher only needed to look towards him in a certain way to make him feel nervous: 'When you get to know someone, you can just look at their face and know what they're thinking.' Extraordinary as it may seem (and it very much upset Mrs K when she heard), Laila and Dave both described slowing down when the teacher told them that they had done something wrong, and they explained that they started to find the teacher's physical appearance frightening *because of the fact she told them that they had done wrong*:

> **Laila:** Well, it's sometimes scary when she says [that you're wrong] ... it's kind of, like, her eyes. When she's looking at your book, like I saw in a film, when she looks up at you, her eyes just look up at you ... [*Laila acts out spooky, scary eyes.*]
>
> **Dave:** And when she looks down at you it's even worse, because her glasses are kind of magnified ... [*Dave demonstrates wide, scary eyes.*]

Aaron described how the teacher's negative feedback to his friend could affect his own learning because he felt more emotionally attached to his friend than to his teacher. He claimed that if the teacher told off a friend, the other children 'kind of slow down because they're so angry with her about [telling off] the other person'.

The children sometimes expressed frustration with the teacher's feedback. Despite being fed up when teachers went 'rah rah rah' and kept repeating themselves (Maddie), they were equally frustrated when they could not remember teacher feedback, because that made it hard to apply. The year 5 boy named Vijay described how hard he found it to keep remembering the teacher's feedback, despite her daily repetitions:

> **EH:** You said every day for a year she's been telling you, 'Don't forget your full stops', something like that?
>
> **Vijay:** Pretty much.
>
> **EH:** It feels like that, anyway? What happens to you when she says that? What do you think or feel?
>
> **Vijay:** I always feel like [*sound of a plane plummeting*].
>
> **EH:** Oops. Yes.
>
> **Vijay:** I always think, 'Maybe I can do it that way tomorrow,' and I always forget overnight.
>
> **EH:** You forget overnight?
>
> **Vijay:** Yeah, my memory's gone a bit bad, but it's getting better. It's coming back.

Vijay did not seem aware that the reason for full stops was that they signalled taking a breath. He seemed to be saying that his aim was to try to remember to carry out the teacher's instructions. And yet, because they had no meaning, no value to him, he struggled constantly to remember. This was a good example of a child with no incentive to pay attention to the teacher's feedback. He was not alone. Generally, the nine children in this study seemed to find teacher feedback frustrating because they perceived it as unrelated to the really valuable aspects of their lives, such as peer–peer relationships, hobbies and fun. The incentive to heed the feedback and then act on it seemed to be largely missing. Here was another good example of the mismatch between the teacher's aims and the pupils' experiences, as described in Chapter 1. They had a sense that what they learned in school had little to do with their *own* values and aspirations, and therefore they need not engage too seriously with their teacher's feedback. If they were not valuing or engaging with this feedback, then there is little puzzle as to why it did not always lead to improvements. Although eight of the nine profiled children said they enjoyed coming to school, none of them gave interest in class-room learning as the reason for enjoying it, and yet from the teacher's perspective, this was the key purpose of school. The children explained quite openly that most learning was unenjoyable and needed to be completed as quickly as possible. Aaron explained that it was normal for children to 'just want to get [classroom learning] over and done with'. Most children primarily liked coming to school because they enjoyed playing with their friends. Mia, a competent, creative middle-class pupil whose mother was a teacher, said she would 'look forward to the breaks'. Mia thought staying in the classroom doing learning was 'kind of wasting our time'. This is not a view that any teacher would be pleased to hear. None the less, these pupils tried obediently to follow instructions in order to 'perform' correctly, in accordance with the teacher's plan. As Fisher's (2011) article suggested, perhaps they were following instructions under a veil of compliance that actually masked significant frustration.

As well, however, as the negative emotions associated with feedback that potentially hindered learning, the children in Emerald Primary School mentioned the positive impact of amusing feedback. Aaron told me that jokey feedback encouraged him to learn, and fortunately Mrs K used humour in her teaching, as many of the pupils agreed. Apparently, 'She has to go in the cupboard and stuff just to laugh!' (Laila). The use of humour in the classroom is unfortunately hugely under-researched and its use in feedback still less researched. But it was clearly important for the children in this study. My informal observation was that humour was also used more among the 'higher' attainers than 'lower' attainers, another shocking finding which, however, made sense to the many teachers I have discussed this with.

As noted in Alex Moore's (2013) research, described in Chapter 1, the children in the current study all felt upset and hard done by because they perceived that the teacher spent more time with every other group than their own. They wanted more of her attention. They seemed to want the teacher who was constantly 'responsive to their individual existence'. In fact, the 'higher' attainers claimed that Mrs K had never sat with them before this research took place, a fact that the teacher acknowledged with a certain mortification.

Children's words: teacher feedback across a whole literacy lesson where the teacher's purposes were at odds with pupils'

One literacy lesson in particular brought home the mismatch between what was going on inside the teacher's mind (Mrs K's) leading to the feedback she gave, compared to the experience of that lesson for two 'lower' attaining pupils, Vijay and Laila. In this lesson, these two pupils were trying hard to engage and were trying to act on the teacher's instructions and feedback. Despite this, it seems likely that their over-riding experience of the lesson was one of frustration and/or confusion because it transpired that the teacher's feedback never managed to respond to some glaring misconceptions that they each held.

Vijay was a small-framed, chatty child who was later diagnosed as dyslexic but at the time of the research was simply portrayed as averse to writing. He came from a relatively unwealthy family, he always seemed to want to please others and had a keen sense of curiosity, especially about historical issues. Laila was a mild, cheerful girl from a relatively well-off family who was usually easy-going but was good at expressing her own opinions, including insightful critical ones.

As prescribed in the National Curriculum and assessed in year 6 national tests at that time, Mrs K was helping the children in year 5 to learn about metaphors, similes, personification, alliteration and rhyme. She seemed to be using a poem called 'From a railway carriage' (by Robert Louis Stevenson) as a text upon which to base her revision about metaphors, similes, personification, alliteration and rhyme. She then used the same poem to draw out her pupils' ideas about historical clues within the poem. The words of the poem were displayed on the class computer screen and they were the only clues provided for the task of working out the historical setting of the poem. The poem concluded with the words 'Here is a cart runaway in the road, Lumping along with man and load; And here is a mill, and there is a river: Each a glimpse and gone forever!'

Mrs K had chosen the 'low' attaining group of pupils to work with. This included Vijay, Laila, Kurt and David. They had falteringly read the poem aloud two lines at a time each, before a short interactive teaching session took place between Mrs K and these four children, in which they focused on metaphors, similes, personification, alliteration and rhyme. As an observer, it was not clear to me that the children understood the poem. It was, however, very clear that they were *not* excited about metaphors, similes, personification, alliteration and rhyme.

At the end of this session, Mrs K asked all the class the question 'When might this poem have been written?' (referring to 'From a Railway Carriage'). She then left these children alone to discuss the question as a small group. The following is the text of the conversation that ensued, in which the children, Laila, David, Vijay and Kurt, were heard negotiating with each other about when the poem might have been written:

David: 19th century time?

Mrs K: Have a talk with each other …

Kurt: In Victoria's reign, more like.

Laila: I don't think it was. I think it was written in, like, 2000.

Vijay: Yeah. Because remember the cha-goo, cha-goo, cha-goo. Remember you need those things on the wheels? Those things? Yeah. Victorian ones didn't have them. They just had the big tank made of steam. So it's after Victorian times.

Kurt: Victorian trains had, like, cogs that worked. They were basic cogs.

Laila: Yeah, but in Victorian [times] it was very rare to go on a train, because you had to be really rich. So not anyone could have written this.

Vijay: They had basic pistons which – you turned the wheels –

David: No, no. You said, remember they usually had those giant tanks? All the water in, then it gets the steam going?

Vijay: Yeah, then the pistons work ...

For this phase of the lesson, Mrs K had suggested that the children act more autonomously, self-directing collaboratively, albeit using rather limited resources. Vijay started working productively, evaluating his efforts by bouncing ideas off peers, especially off David and Kurt who were fellow historic engine enthusiasts. A thoughtful and constructive dialogue emerged among his group, in which each child's contribution built in some way on the contribution of the previous speaker, although there was also evidence of discord and discontinuity.

In retrospect, it is possible to understand Laila's puzzling comments about the poem being written in modern times. This was, it transpired later, because she saw that the poem had been presented on the computer. She therefore assumed that it must be as modern as computers are. And she knew that computers were a relatively new invention. Laila was therefore trying her hardest to apply historical knowledge to the poem as Mrs K had instructed, but drawing on a particular and misguided set of data which Mrs K did not know about. Vijay and Laila's conversation during our post-observation interview later that day was enlightening and threw up even more misconceptions:

EH: So the question of when it was written, I think you found that quite hard, didn't you?

[*Neither child responds to this meta-question, preferring to try again to solve the actual problem.*]

Laila: I thought it was more modern, because you couldn't really have done it in the Victorian era. Because you had to pay a lot of money to go on the trains. I thought it might have been 1993 or it could have been 2000.

EH: Why in particular those years?

Vijay: [*incredulous*] 1993?

Laila: Why?

Vijay: That's only a few years ago.

Laila: I know.

EH: So why did you pick on those years? I'm interested.

Laila: Because there was world war, but you couldn't – there was a bit of a panic in world war.

[Laila has now moved her argument away from wealth to her well-evidenced knowledge about life during the Second World War. Her argument still leads to her conclusion that the poem must be modern but she is not yet expressing her biggest confusion about the presence of the computer. She seems to be holding three theories simultaneously in her mind.]

Vijay: That was only seventeen years ago, 1993.

EH: The world war was a bit before that, wasn't it?

Laila: And if you think about it, all of that space and time, I couldn't really imagine – well, because there were loads of bomb sites in the world war.

Vijay: *[interrupting]* Yes, but, he could have been an evacuee.

[Vijay is now displaying his own well-evidenced knowledge about life during the war but abandoning his evidence relating to train engines.]

Laila: – and there were loads of carriages, but you did say about carriages, they were a big thing in Victorian times. So it couldn't have been during the war.

[Laila seems to be struggling here and losing faith in her own reasoning. She is now entertaining a fourth theory.]

EH: I agree with you.

Vijay: Cart, cart, carriage.

EH: The 'cart' is a bit of a clue.

Laila: *[Laila seems to think that EH is suggesting that the presence of the 'cart' indicates that the poem is old. Once again, Laila is drawing on her everyday knowledge, correctly.]*

Yeah, but it could be – we still have carts around here.

Vijay: *[referring to his go-kart]* My cart.

EH: And you were going to say it was from Victorian times, because ...?

Vijay: Train rides. And I also thought that it was partly from the world war as well.

[It seems that Vijay is toying with two feasible alternatives; it is not clear how the 'cart' self-directed talk fitted into these.]

EH: Why is that?

Vijay: Because he could have been going to the country.

EH: Oh, an evacuee, from the city. That is perfectly possible.

Vijay: Which reminds me that my granddad, which is still alive, and my dad's proper dad, he was an evacuee. And my granddad who is, you know, sort of a divorce type of granddad, he's dead, he died at eighty, but he was a Desert Rat.

[Vijay's keen sense of history starts to come to life again here. In fact, he seems more interested in his own historical knowledge than the answer the teacher had asked for.]

Laila: What's a Desert Rat?

[Laila seems genuinely interested and perhaps she is hoping that his answer will shed light on her confusion.]

EH: Tell Laila what a Desert Rat is.

Vijay: A Desert Rat is someone – sort of taking different parts of the army – I think because it's *Desert* Rat, they sort of took bits of the British Army and bits of the German Army to a desert and fought there.

Laila: I don't understand why it could be Victorian.

[Disappointed in Vijay's explanation, Laila seems determined to get this straight in her mind. She is not happy to let it go. Now she is getting to the most urgent confusion in her mind.]

EH: You don't understand?

Laila: There's a big space gap. Huge.

EH: There's a big gap between the Victorians and the world war.

[But Laila is presumably thinking of the gap between Victorian times, or war time, and the invention of the computer.]

Vijay: Big, big, big. World war was something like seventy, sixty years ago.

EH: It was the early forties.

Laila: And they didn't really have a lot of paper and pens and stuff.

EH: They did in world war times. Victorian times they might have written in ink pen, mightn't they?

Laila: Yeah, but how could they get it up to a website? It was on a website on the board.

[Now Laila's main misconception is becoming clear.]

Vijay: But really old paper is just made of strips of tree bark.

[Vijay seems to be enjoying incorporating more of his everyday knowledge rather than following Laila's line of thinking.]

It is perhaps sobering to now review the feedback session that followed the actual class relating to 'From a Railway Carriage'. It is sobering to return to this having jumped forward in time to the post-lesson interview in which Laila and Vijay's misconceptions and contributions were revealed. They were living with these misconceptions and holding onto these potential contributions during the class time in which the teacher, Mrs K, gave feedback on the whole lesson, including feedback on the group discussions about the date of the poem. Here is the transcript of the plenary feedback session following the small group discussions:

Teacher: Okay. Which kind of leads us, I guess, to our question number two, when do you think it was written? I think I agree with Maddie, by the way. It's a steam train. Yeah. There's something in the words, as well, that might make you say 'Oh, it's not a train that, for example, you might sit on now to go to London.' Why it's obvious that that's not a South-West or a Southern or whatever train, trains that go up to London [from Surrey]? ... So I'm thinking that what you'd see out of the window would be very different, wouldn't it, when you're on a steam train which was ... whenever, again, however many years it's going to be. What might you see out of a train window now? Cities. What else might you see? Laila?

Laila: Loads of buildings and blocks of flats.

[Laila is directly answering Mrs K's question rather than linking this to her conceptions about how modern the poem is.]

Teacher: Yeah. Houses. Blocks of flats. It doesn't mention that, you see? Buildings, offices, you might see. What else might you see? Yes, I know, you might go through the countryside, you might see similar things, but what else might you see near? Hands up if you've been on a train. Right, so let's have some ideas, then. Aurelia, what might you see through the window of a train?

[Pause]

Aurelia: Tunnels?

[Aurelia's answer does not seem to be the one Mrs K is looking for.]

Teacher: Yes, tunnels, maybe them as well. Josh?

Josh: Nothing if you're on the tube.

Teacher: *[laughs]* Yes. Okay. Thank you very much. Nothing if you're on the tube. ... Andrea?

Andrea: Roads?

Teacher: Yes! That's what I'm thinking! *[Now the 'right' answer has been given.]* And what goes on roads?

Sarah: Cars.

Teacher: Yes. *[It seems that in Mrs K's mind, the fact that there are no cars in the poem suggests that it is very old.]* So when do you think this poem was written? What do you think? Vijay, what do you think?

Vijay: I think it's kind of mixed in with Victoria's reign and the war.

Teacher: *[Mrs K seems **not** to have heard the second part of Vijay's sentence 'and the war'.]* Lovely. Hands up if you agree with Vijay: some time in the Victorian years? Yeah. So anyone know … 1890, something like that? *[Mrs K now gives the answer.]*

My purpose in providing excerpts from this whole three-part sequence is to illustrate the role that the teacher's feedback played and to give some insight about what was meanwhile going on for the two children, Vijay and Laila. During the group discussion section, the children's rich everyday knowledge was demonstrated and they drew on their autonomy to tackle the challenge she set them; but their differences and questions were not addressed by the teacher, either at this stage or later. The post-lesson interview data, which I gathered during interview with just Laila and Vijay later that day, again demonstrated both their substantial everyday knowledge but also their extreme confusion. This confusion seemed to frustrate Laila more than it did Vijay. During this interview, Laila finally exposed her fundamental misassumption about computers not existing in Victorian times. Vijay's confusion as to whether this poem was written in Victorian times or during the Second World War was never unravelled; however, this did not seem to bother him so much. He was anyway enjoying the opportunity for talking about historical events he knew about.

The final classroom plenary feedback session illustrated how the two children's misconceptions and questions were still not picked up, and indeed, the teacher (unintentionally) ignored Vijay's expression of confusion. None of the everyday knowledge that they had both brought to the session is fed back on, and the active inquiry session that happened earlier seemed to be contradicted by the teacher providing answers herself rather than asking for a range of solutions and reasons for each one. Of course, Mrs K was surely under pressure of time and an overloaded curriculum. The aim here is not to blame her. Indeed, one would need to discuss her plans and experiences in detail with her in order to make any judgements. However, the extracts do, I think, point to the lost learning potential of these two keen, curious pupils which could have been more fruitfully harnessed through a different model of teacher feedback.

Children's words: young children critiqued the teacher's overly directive feedback

In the UK, a government-advocated synthetic phonics-based literacy program, Read Write Inc. (RWI), was introduced in many primary schools across the country in an attempt to boost literacy levels in younger students. Teacher-researcher and then-MA student Luke Rolls considered the scheme to be very prescriptive in terms of teacher input and was interested to explore what *implications* this prescriptiveness had for teacher feedback during the process. He explored to what extent feedback in a scheme like RWI could be adapted in order to promote children's proactive engagement and self-direction (autonomous learning).

Luke Rolls noted the inherent need for students to be provoked to interact with, assimilate, interpret and/or accommodate information in feedback, rather than just carry out instructions. He believed that a crucial part of feedback was not just the explicit subject-content of the feedback message, but also the implicit messages sent within the feedback about the nature of learning and how much control learners have over directing it. Rolls was particularly interested in the relationship between feedback and the development of a 'growth mindset' (Dweck, 2006) whereby pupils valued the process of directing their own learning and determining its outcomes.

Rolls' study, based on this theoretical framework, took place in a mixed year 1 and 2 literacy group (ages 5–6) of around 20 students at an east London school situated in an area of socio-economic deprivation. Around ten audio recordings were taken of daily lessons over the period of one month, alongside several video recordings of parts of lessons. A post-study interview was carried out to elicit student views on different aspects of feedback.

In the list of *steps* below, by 'Prescribed feedback methods', Rolls referred to guidance given in the 'RWI Phonics Handbook' and 'Speed Sounds Lesson Plans' and as delivered by RWI school training consultants (Miskin, 2006a, 2006b). By 'Adapted feedback method', he referred to the feedback approaches that he himself tried to use in order ultimately to promote more proactive engagement and self-direction, or learning autonomy, among pupils. He called his adapted feedback *facilitative* (see Black and Wiliam, 2006) implying that the child was facilitated to interact with, assimilate, interpret and/or accommodate the feedback information. This is akin to *provocative* feedback and is contrasted with 'directive' feedback whereby the teacher simply told pupils what to do.

Step 1: Prescribed feedback method
In practising letter sounds at the beginning of each lesson, the teacher gives corrective feedback to students based on the accuracy of their pronunciation of the graphemes exercise.

Adapted feedback method
Students are given exemplars of accurate and inaccurate pronunciations of letter sounds based on common misconceptions. Through self and peer assessment, students listen out to identify sounds and are given a signal to communicate their responses. In a mastery-type game, the class strive to improve at fluency and speed.

Step 2: Prescribed feedback method
Based on the focus 'sound of the day', children practise applying their phonetic knowledge to spelling words on mini-whiteboards. The teacher will ask children to show their whiteboards together and then give corrective feedback around the accuracy of the spellings.

Adapted feedback method

Rather than simultaneously showing the teacher their mini-whiteboard spelling attempts, children are encouraged to try assessing for themselves the accuracy of their spellings and are corrected through facilitative feedback. A more subtle facilitative *cue* is given at first to a child that incorrectly spells a word. If this is not taken up, a more directive prompt is used.

Step 3: Prescribed feedback method

In pairs, children help their partner to practise saying the letter sounds, decode focus words and read a short book using 'point, help, praise'. Students are encouraged to 'praise' their partner with phrases like 'super sounds!' to motivate them.

Adapted feedback method

To practise focus sounds and words, student pairs are given a choice of several pointing games. In daily discussion, the class discusses both the social/emotional aspects of feedback and its cognitive function.

Step 4: Prescribed feedback method

During the comprehension-focused part of the lesson, the teacher gives students questions around the content of the book. These are divided into recall ('find it') and inference-type ('prove it') questions. Feedback is gained from the children through eliciting choral, paired or individual responses to questions.

Adapted feedback method

In a circle, the children sit and individually think of a question they would like to ask the class relating to the events or characters in the story. Certain conventions are established before children pose their questions; for example, students address the person they are speaking to in a friendly voice while everyone else actively listens.

Step 5: Prescribed feedback method

Students use a success criteria checklist written next to their piece of writing, with prompts to check when self-assessing their work. The given success criteria are the same in all student books, so teacher feedback needs to address individual learning needs.

Adapted feedback method

Students are encouraged to reflect in their writing on their learning goals and develop their own personally adapted success criteria. At the end of a written piece, students indicate a plus (+), equals (=) or minus (−) sign to show whether they think their writing was an improvement, equivalent or a regression on previous attempts. Next to a + self-assessment, students write a justification as to what had made it a more successful piece.

Luke Rolls described the following findings after trying out his 'adapted' feedback approaches.

A balance was required between directive and facilitative feedback

Students expressed a preference for facilitative (provocative) rather than directive (descriptive) feedback. The more facilitative approach appeared to foster self-direction in students. It became clear, however, that 'facilitative' feedback by itself was not always functioning accessibly for a few students who seemed to find open-ended cues too subtle to be of use when self-assessing a spelling or a letter formation, for example. If singularly pursued with these students, rather than promoting learning autonomy, such feedback may have simply served to encode failure. This suggests that student task performance may relate to an optimum degree of autonomy, but this tipping point may vary between students or groups of students. Most other students, who appeared to have greater self-direction capacities, reacted well to higher levels of facilitative feedback. Rolls followed the pattern, throughout the study, of offering facilitative feedback in the first instance, attempting to nurture students' active self-direction, and resorting to directive feedback when required. In the post-study interview, a debate between a few of the students picked up on the tension between the two types of feedback and the development of autonomy. They questioned the efficacy of just 'being told' by the teacher:

> **Valerie:** [Up to now] the teacher is going to tell you what is wrong when you show the boards, but when you check yourself, you go through it and you see the mistakes [by yourself].
>
> **Miya:** I think it's both: because what if you have to write 'was' and you write 'woz', and then you're like, right I'm just gonna tick it off. It's good for the teacher to tell you, because you may have made a mistake.
>
> **Hannah:** No, then you won't learn anything.
>
> **Miya:** No, you will, your brain grows because you've made a mistake.
>
> **LR:** Perhaps you can learn in either situation, but which one is better?
>
> **Miya:** I still think both. They don't know half of it – [with the teacher's help], they can realise it.
>
> **Hannah:** I think the teacher shouldn't tell you because it's better to do it by yourself because if the teacher told you the answer you might not learn anything.

Nicol and Macfarlane-Dick (2006, p.9) acknowledged Miya's idea: 'Teachers are much more effective in identifying errors or misconceptions in students' work than peers or the students themselves. In effect, feedback from teachers can help substantiate student self-regulation.' For students displaying less self-direction, teacher directive feedback did appear to support the development of their self-direction, but the initial facilitative cues were nevertheless possibly helpful for them to start engaging with the problem. An encouraging development was that for nearly all students, the need for directive feedback decreased over time and although working from different starting points, these children did appear to gradually improve in their capacity for helping themselves.

Engaging students in dialogue shaped a co-constructed approach to feedback

In consultation with the class about the format of different sections of the lessons, Rolls negotiated how collaborative learning activities should be done, and what praise, if any, might be used. Such negotiation was reportedly favoured by all students and appeared to contribute to a sense of competence, autonomy *and* relatedness as pupils directed their learning in collaboration with others. In the post-study interview, several of the children were critical of other phonics groups they had been in. They expressed clear opinions about having had a lack of autonomy and choice during their earlier learning experiences. Several children seemed to be showing first signs of critical inquiry, challenging their past encounters of learning the subject.

Non-participation in class discussions was, however, an issue when inviting more introverted students to contribute. Voting for one of a few choices was one way they could express their opinions, but full equity in gauging student 'voice' was difficult to achieve.

Developing a 'growth mindset' in students was associated with increased persistence in learning

Rolls reported that some students at the beginning of the study appeared to display characteristics of a performance-orientation in their approach to learning. That is, they appeared more interested in getting approval for a right answer than in their own process of arriving at the right answer. Inspired by the work of Dweck (2006), Rolls specifically introduced the children to how the brain grows when more challenging learning material is experienced. He tried to develop a class ethos which emphasised success being 'due to internal, unstable, specific factors such as effort' (Black and Wiliam, 2006, p.12). Students appeared enthused and fascinated (in simple terms) by the idea that a brain synapse connects when a mistake is subsequently understood.

This change was expressed by students' exclamations in the recordings, where Rolls heard children declaring, for example 'I love the tricky ones'. This way of thinking culminated in the class request in the last lesson to attempt to spell the word:

antidisestablishmentarianism.

Children seemed to create more adventurous sentences in the writing part of the lesson.

Effective peer feedback was reliant on kind, cooperative and inclusive interactions

Collaborative feedback exchanges were generally challenging to optimise (as depicted in Chapter 2). Students said that they had had past negative experiences of receiving feedback from partners which may have compounded the difficulty. Students gradually came to an agreement that it was how feedback was communicated that was important for them:

> **LR:** Does anyone feel annoyed with your partner when they teach you? Like, 'Don't tell me what to do ...'?
>
> **Kai:** If they say 'purh', but she says that's not 'purh' it's 'p'. I feel, eh, stop being rude.
>
> **LR:** Yeah, is it rude ...? If she's trying to teach you?
>
> **Kai:** [It is ...] because she's saying it in a rude way.

Perhaps as a result of this, the majority of the class felt that praise from a partner was helpful. In fact, all kind, magnanimous interactions did appear to have a positive impact on their collaborative learning. Overall, reciprocal student-led questioning appeared to increase group engagement in discussion. However, in terms of increasing participation, a combination of both talk-partners and whole-class dialogue appeared to be most beneficial. This seemed to allow more introverted children to readily contribute in their pairs, where they would not in a large group, as well as afford them the opportunity to engage in peripheral learning, listening to and learning from the ideas of others.

Self-regulatory and peer-led feedback

Students were asked to reflect on and justify their reasoning for any self-assessments they made by explaining the quality of their writing. Some of the students additionally demonstrated that they could take control over their own quality assurance procedures:

> **Hannah:** I write the + [mark – to indicate improvement], but before I do, I check my work again to make sure and then I tick it, read it back again. I do check from the day before. I read the sentence from yesterday and then decide whether it is the same or better [than today]. Yes, then the next day, I do try to see what I need to improve on.
>
> **Miya:** I really try hard to decide which one is better [yesterday's or today's]. I'm like, 'Oh I need to be careful!' and each day I'm trying to get better and better.
>
> **Hannah:** Writing 'because' next to your +/=/− is good because it helps the teacher know why you wrote plus, equals or minus.

Valerie: I think it helps not just us, but the teacher too because we are not making loads and loads of mistakes and they don't have to correct a lot. If the teacher is always 'Oh, check your full-stop! Oh, check your capital letter! Oh, where's your finger spaces? Oh, where's your wow words?', then the children won't learn and the teacher will be the one who always has to correct it.

ACTIVITIES FOR CLASSROOM PRACTICE: SOME PRACTICAL WAYS FORWARD FOR TEACHERS AND OTHER EDUCATORS IN CLASSROOMS

Discussion or journal writing

With a partner or in a private learning journal, describe your worst ever experience of 'receiving feedback'. What made it so bad?

Next, describe the feedback you remember that has most helped your learning. What made it so helpful?

Now consider the children's voices about feedback, as presented above. Focus especially on:

- the difference in how children experience evaluative, descriptive and provocative feedback respectively;

- the potential damage to children and their learning that can be caused by evaluative or self-directed feedback;

- the relationship between the teacher's feedback and children's sense of autonomy;

- differences between teachers' and pupils' perceptions about feedback; and

- the dangers of overly-prescriptive feedback.

Actions to try out

Try asking pupils to tell each other about and to record for the teacher their worst and best experiences of feedback in the classroom.

What happens when the teacher only gives encouraging and/or provocative feedback in the classroom (i.e. no routine praise, no correction, nothing negative)?

Keep a tally of how often teacher feedback focuses on the child being correct rather than the child using well-selected strategies.

Plenary

Describe, reflect on and analyse for yourself or in a pair/group, what happened when these actions were tried out in classrooms.

How will you engage pupils in evaluating any of the ideas you have tried out?

5

Social class in the classroom

> ❝ People laughed at me every single day for two weeks [for being in the 'lowest' group] ... it was me and Yvonne who were treated like **nothing**. (Curtis, year 6) ❞

Chapters 1 to 4 have made connections between children having a voice in the classroom (Chapter 1) and children's autonomy in learning (Chapter 3). Chapter 2 illustrated how children's autonomy and their capacity to nurture it were restricted by a long-standing culture of authoritarianism in classrooms the world over. In these, pupils have little say over their classroom learning, they have limited autonomy and they tend to feel fear, all of which have clear negative effects on learning autonomy. In Chapter 4, children's words were presented which suggested that the teacher's feedback could encourage or inhibit their sense of autonomy in the classroom and it could affect children's experience of being heard, with subsequent influences on learning. Chapter 5 now investigates a potential further obstacle to children's sense of autonomy in the classroom: social class. Drawing particularly on the work of Diane Reay, it considers how children from homes with lower socio-economic status may find additional barriers to their autonomy and to their voices being heard.

Social disadvantage and schooling: a segregated system

> Regardless of what individual working-class males and females are able to negotiate and achieve for themselves within education, the collective patterns of working-class trajectories remain sharply different from those of the middle-classes, despite over a hundred years of state schooling. (Reay, 2012, p.294)

Many authors would agree that classrooms are partly responsible for the increasing difference between the post-school experiences of working-class pupils and those of middle-class pupils. Steve Strand (2014) has reported that at age 16, the achievement gap associated with social class was twice as large as the biggest ethnic gap and six times as large as the gender gap. Children from high socio-economic status (SES) homes are 50 per cent more likely to stay in education after 16 than their low SES counterparts (Reay, 2006, p.291).

What is even more shocking is that UK schools have been recently described in an OECD report as the 'most socially segregated' in the developed world (OECD, 2010), which highlights the fact that disadvantaged children are concentrated together in schools, despite the nominally 'comprehensive' nature of the schooling system. This OECD report claimed that the figures for the UK were also part of a bigger international picture of a growing divide between the educational 'haves' and 'have nots'. However, although more young people than ever before have got into university in the UK (until tuition fees were imposed, at least), the proportion of young people not in education, employment or training is also well above the OECD average.

Working-class school pupils (from low SES backgrounds) attain fewer qualifications than their middle-class peers (from high SES backgrounds) (Dunne and Gazeley, 2008). The fewer qualifications of working-class students have been partly explained by the Bow Group, who suggested that in 2007, for example, nearly 60,000 pupils in the UK did not obtain any GCSEs, either through not turning up to their GCSE exams, not passing any exams, not being entered for GCSE exams, or disappearing off the school roll (Skidmore et al., 2007). The figures indicated the consistently failing 'tail' of UK secondary schools which implied that at least for this section of the population, mainly made up of working-class students, classrooms held little promise for future well-being in any of the four senses outlined by Schiro (2013) as proposed purposes for state schooling (see Chapter 1). In other words, for many pupils from homes with low SES, classrooms have not transferred to them the traditional knowledge of their society; nor have they equipped them adequately for employment; nor led them to be flourishing, well-rounded individuals; nor allowed them to confront effectively social inequalities within existing society.

The clear social differences between working-class and middle-class children in schools were also made transparent in Alice Sullivan et al.'s (2014, p.750) study of the 1970 British Cohort followed through to the present day. They noted that 31 per cent of privately educated cohort members achieved an elite degree, compared to 13 per cent of grammar pupils, 5 per cent of comprehensive pupils and 2 per cent of secondary modern pupils – the latter two school-types being where working-class pupils have tended to cluster.

These factors affect the life chances of the less qualified students and often lead them into unskilled, poorly paid jobs or no employment at all (Barbeau et al., 2004); they may lead to poorer health and/or an increased tendency towards crime (Rogalsky, 2009). The nature of the labour market also has a powerful effect on the incentive structures confronting learners in classrooms (Keep, 2009). The prevalence of low-paid, low-skilled work is liable to generate weak incentives to learn for those who believe themselves destined to enter such employment (and who consider the purpose of schooling to be preparation for employment). As numbers of those who attend universities have increased, there has grown evidence of the occupational filtering down of graduates, and also indications that employers were usually failing to upgrade their jobs to take advantage of graduates' capabilities. Therefore, even those who graduate from universities, if they end up as over-qualified and under-appreciated, this seems to have a long-term scarring effect on wage levels, as well as on job satisfaction (Green et al., 2012). Moreover, a surplus of better qualified young people is displacing those who hold less good qualifications, many of them working-class, but who are still perfectly capable of doing the job (UKCES, 2012, p. 6).

In-work poverty has grown in the last decade by 20 per cent, and in 2012 there were claimed to be over six million people living in low income households. Tom MacInnes and colleagues (2013) found that over 50 per cent of the 13 million people in the UK living in poverty were in a working family. There were also indications that employment in low-skilled occupations was growing, and that the recession and high unemployment have combined to encourage and enable employers to further casualise work, for example through zero and limited hours contracts, and to downgrade the terms and conditions of employment.

Such research indicates that while human capital (in the form of certain types and levels of qualification, gained from certain kinds of institution) will get a person onto the employment race track, it is class, gender and ethnicity-based forms of social and cultural capital that will thereafter tend to determine who wins the top spots. This means that even at the level of gaining employment using 'formal' qualifications tested against traditional subject-knowledge as success criteria, social class tends to play a discriminatory role. Moreover, the emphasis some employers place on recruiting on the basis of 'soft' skills (such as particular ways of communicating) may work to the disadvantage of those from lower socio-economic backgrounds, as the soft skills being sought are often a proxy for class attributes.

Definitions of 'working class'

Recently I asked Jessica, a teacher who worked in a struggling inner-city secondary school, 'Are most of your students working class?'. She looked at me in disbelief for a few seconds and then replied, 'None of them are working class. Most of their parents have never been able to find any work.' The students that Jessica taught were a particular section of the 'working class' in that one can assume they would have been 'working class' if they had found work.

By 'working class' in terms of employment, I use David Barbeau et al.'s (2004) definition, which combines the individual's relative employment *position* with the *nature* of their employment. By this definition, it is meaningful to claim that a working-class adult who does have employment will be engaging in semi-routine or routine work rather than in managerial or professional work. It could also be claimed that they carry out 'blue-collar' tasks or act as service workers. A substantial proportion of working-class people in England, whether in or out of employment, are also from ethnic minority groups. The working-class adult is less likely to have a university degree, as explained above.

However, class manifests itself differently in different international contexts. For example, teacher-researcher and MA-student Wan Ju asked pupils in Taiwan from poor (working-class) families how they perceived middle-class people, and they responded as follows (translated from Mandarin):

> Noble!
>
> Rich!
>
> They have great power!
>
> The lower-class *have to* take their tip!
>
> They can command the lower-class.

These quotations not only emphasise the money and social position the middle-class were perceived to have, but also refer to the power relations between middle- and working-class people. In fact, it was noticeable to Wan Ju that some students seemed to consider it *natural* that the working-classes served the middle-classes.

Middle-class views of working-class pupils

How the middle-class regards the working-class is the subject of this next section because of the potential negative influences this regard can impose. Diane Reay (2005) has suggested exploring these negative influences at two levels:

> I need more understanding of how social class is actually lived, of how it informs my inner worlds *to complement research* on how it shapes my life chances in the outer world. (p.913, my emphasis)

This next section aims to explore the first level: how social class is actually experienced within the classroom by pupils. One recurrent theme is the poor sense of self that some working-class pupils evidently build up of themselves in classrooms, sensing that they have limited value and that their voice is not important within the social world of the classroom. Such pupils do not feel treated as competent and maturely responsible people. These factors can lead to diminished, even miserable, experiences in classrooms for working-class pupils. Diane Reay commented that this phenomenon was not helped by the fact that middle-class people tended to view the working-class in a negative fashion, as made up of individuals who needed to take more responsibility for their lives. The title of a recent book, *Chavs: The Demonization of the Working-Class* (Jones, 2011), gave a flavour of this negativity. The book itself revealed, among other things, the power of middle-class journalists to portray people from the working-class in a particular, largely negative, light.

Working-class pupils might be living with deeply embedded feelings of shame, fear, envy and resentment (Reay, 2005, 2012) and feelings of inferiority, dependence, anxiety and unhappiness (Rogalsky, 2009) as a result of their social positioning in the classroom, in relation to the middle-class children (whether within the same school or segregated schools). Recent research has suggested that, not only are working-class students more likely to attend poor-quality schools and experience pedagogies that are less stimulating, exciting or challenging (Francis and Mills, 2012), but in addition to that, they tend to be considered less able by teachers, given less positive feedback and moved to lower 'ability' classes or groups within classrooms, sometimes regardless of their potential (Reay, 2006, 2012; also see below on the relationship between social class and 'ability' groups).

Current research has suggested that school staff may unwittingly meet the needs of students from their own cultural backgrounds (i.e. usually middle class) better than of those from other backgrounds (Dunne and Gazeley, 2008). Working-class students' identity has tended to be undervalued in school classrooms, often being associated in a reductionist manner with lack of 'ability' per se (Reay, 2012). On the basis of 'contractual benevolence', middle-class operators may have expected working-class participants to accept their own dominant values gratefully (Gause, 2011). School rules too have reflected middle-class ideas about 'proper' behaviour and manners, sometimes without recognition that these may not be valued equivalently within working-class culture. Even school uniforms have embodied class-based (as well as gender-based) definitions of taste and appropriate behaviour (Raby, 2012).

Marie-Christine Opdenakker and Jan Van Damme (2000, p.183) illustrated how common classroom discipline structures were often damaging for children from less educationally motivated families, often working-class families. Testing and categorising regimes in particular have increased the perceived low status of working-class pupils whose talents and aspirations may not fit these models (Reay, 2012). Diane Reay suggested that one consequence of the growing preoccupations with testing and assessment led to a *fixing* of failure in the working-classes. Like pupil Curtis (above) who felt like a 'nothing', Reay described how working-class girls mentioned being 'rubbish' and 'no good', and she concluded that some lived 'without a self':

> These girls, in the context of schooling, inhabit a psychic economy of class defined by fear, anxiety and unease where failure looms large and success is elusive ... without a self. (2006, p.299)

Children's sense of being valued and respected as competent and maturely responsible in the classroom is key to both formal attainment and to more general well-being, as suggested in Chapters 2–4 of this book. Dimpna Devine's (2003) study in Irish primary schools unearthed that children from working-class families were typified as being not interested in education whereas children from middle-class backgrounds were exemplified in terms of their ambition to succeed and get the most from the system. Children were aware of these assumptions and their social position in the classroom and school; they were able to recognise the power relations and to identify the dominant/dominated voices. Reay has argued that the ways in which power was distributed within classrooms inevitably silenced certain groups of students, usually those with lower SES backgrounds. Therefore, the experience of being a pupil means different things for pupils who are positioned in different social categories in the classroom. And usually the experience is more negative if you are working-class.

Classroom influences on pupils' experience of the classroom

The classroom is likely to influence pupils' sense of self – being valued as competent and maturely responsible people – in particular through the following dimensions:

1. How teachers and peers talk about pupils in relation to their social class, 'ability', race, gender, performance and appearance

The teachers' off-the-cuff comments in the classroom ('She won't be able to achieve that. No-one off that estate goes far'), can reinforce social class stereotypes, often in combination with racial and gender stereotypes. Teachers' derogatory references to the 'ability' performance and/or appearance of working-class pupils can reinforce stereotypes and undermine social equality in the classroom.

2. Opportunities provided by teachers for pupils to express their own voices especially in dialogue

Speech is a key indicator of social class whereby working-class pupils may use different words or registers than their teachers or middle-class peers (see Streib, 2011). Middle-class pupils tend to have more practice in using complex language and may inadvertently use up more classroom air-time than their working-class colleagues. This may lead to the teacher not asking those who speak less or differently to contribute so often, thus disadvantaging these pupils further. However, as outlined above, when school classrooms do not support inclusive participation, and even make it more difficult for working-class students, their chances of well-being in the future may be compromised.

3. Encouragement by teachers and peers for pupils taking risks and assuming mature responsibilities

There is evidence that, because they are different and often assumed to be less 'able' than their middle-class counterparts, teachers unwittingly spoon-feed and direct working-class students more than middle-class students even though, outside school, working-class students may be expected to be more maturely responsible and 'streetwise' than their middle-class peers (see also evidence of this in Emerald Primary School, Chapter 3, where less autonomy was encouraged among 'low' attainers, who tended to include mainly working-class pupils).

4. Expectations expressed by teachers that subject knowledge is both useful and manageable for all pupils

Assumptions underpinning school curricula, especially when approached from Schiro's (2013) first philosophical sense, 'to help children learn the accumulated knowledge of our culture: that of the academic disciplines', may place inappropriate demands on working-class pupils whose representatives may not have contributed to deciding on the content of the curriculum. Content that seems essential to the middle-class teacher or parent may seem irrelevant or even destructive to some working-class students: for example, learning mainly about kings and queens and wars in history lessons; focusing on metaphors, similes and alliteration during English lessons.

On the other hand, for some working-class students, school is the only place where they can learn certain skills and approaches because they tend to have fewer opportunities at home and have parents who are less skilled in 'pushing' their children into the best situations (Nandy, 2012). Teachers and other pupils therefore have a prime opportunity to affect each other's knowledge positively.

5. Links made by teachers explicitly to pupils' own lives and others' lives beyond the classroom.

It may be harder for middle-class teachers to relate to the lives of working-class children, drawing on examples from these pupils' lifestyles. Lack of links to the working-class child's life outside the classroom might exacerbate the distance between home and school and increase the likelihood that schooling seems irrelevant. As Erica Nordlander and her colleagues (2015) suggested, *those with support systems outside the classroom were likely to be less affected by negatively experienced events within the classroom.* In other words, pupils who shared the (middle-class) networks and assumptions of those who ran schools and classrooms were likely to thrive better than those by whom such networks and assumptions have to be consciously cultivated (Pryor and Crossouard, 2008). This is what Reay referred to as the 'unacknowledged normality of the middle-classes ... and its corollary, the equally unacknowledged pathologisation and diminishment of the working-classes' (Reay, 2006, p.289).

Children's words: working-class pupils noticed the teacher's differentiated treatment according to social class

One pupil commented pertinently in Burke and Grosvenor's (2003) study:

> The children who do well in exams think they're better than the kids who can't read! Surely I can't go on thinking like that! (p.62)

Drawing on considerations such as those listed above, Diane Reay (2006) specifically asked pupils whether they felt they had the confidence to act; whether they felt that they belonged within the school community; whether they felt they had the power to influence the procedures and practices which shaped their learning. In response, she described how working-class pupils talked about 'a sense of educational worthlessness and feeling that they were not really valued and respected within education' (p.297). One boy, Kenny, was quoted as telling the teachers:

> You don't need to love us. All you need to do is treat us like humans.

Neil added:

> It's like they think you're stupid or something.

These quotations bear reflection. Their meaning is devastatingly clear: these pupils did not feel respected or valued by their teachers.

The girls in that class, while less vociferous, also embodied a 'potent sense of unfairness and unequal treatment' by their teachers, because of their social class (p.298). Reay cited the following conversation among the girls:

> **Jenna:** Yeah, our English teacher. He likes the three clever [middle-class] girls a lot because they are always answering questions. He never gives other people a chance to say ...
>
> **Sarah:** If we put our hands up and we want to answer the question, the cleverest person, he will ask them, and we all know it's the right answer. And then he starts shouting at us saying that we are not answering.
>
> **Alex:** Yeah, and like, with them [middle-class] lot as well, if they ask to sit next to their friends they get to sit next to their friends.
>
> **Sharmaine:** And we're split up and made to sit with boys.
>
> **Sarah:** Yeah, but it's just them three particular [middle-class] girls, they get to always sit where they want to sit.

Another of Diane Reay's studies (in 1995) compared a middle-class UK primary school with a working-class one. She found that, sometimes, middle-class pupils were allowed to give advice, such as recommending a maths book or redesigning class assemblies. The teacher, perhaps eager to embody democratic values in her classroom, would follow this advice. As Reay interpreted this, the middle-class children were in this way 'constructing themselves as "equals" of the teachers' (1995, p.364), which both made them feel authoritative and also reinforced their (superior) social class position. Reay did not, however, find any evidence of the working-class children in her study doing this. It appeared that the working-class pupils had less confidence to act and felt they had less power to influence the procedures and practices which shaped their learning (i.e. less sense of their own authority).

The links between social class and 'ability' groups in classrooms

In the section on middle-class views of working-class pupils (above), it was suggested that working-class pupils often ended up in so-called low 'ability' groups mainly on the basis of their social class. Diane Reay (2006) described how 'low ability' and 'lower-class' tended to become conflated (see also Gillborn and Youdell, 2000):

> The pupils in the bottom sets were exclusively working-class ... contributing to processes of contemporary educational governance that literally fix failure in the working-classes, while simultaneously fixing them in devalued educational spaces. (p.298)

Despite Gordon Stobart's (2014) call to challenge 'the myth of ability', so-called 'ability' grouping has become almost taken for granted in both primary and secondary schools in England, even at Key Stage 1 (ages 5–7). The word 'ability' is often used in classrooms in the absurdly outdated sense of denoting something inherent in the child like having a certain colour of eyes. As young teacher-researcher and MA-student Sean Macnamara wrote (personal correspondence, June 2016):

> There are teachers, myself included, who have only ever known a curriculum that groups pupils by 'ability', having experienced being grouped by 'ability' themselves as pupils; and now grouping pupils by 'ability' in their own classrooms. 'Ability' grouping seems to be accepted as the norm and expectation in most primary school classrooms. Having looked at the [research] literature and concluded that it is overwhelmingly in support of mixed 'ability' teaching – with evidence for the effectiveness of 'ability' grouping extremely limited – this makes for a curious situation. How is the gap between academic research and classroom practice so vast?

There are many answers to this very pertinent question which are in fact relevant to this chapter. Tammy Campbell (2014) pointed out the British government's role in the promotion of 'ability' grouping in England. Consecutive (right/centre) governments have claimed to be eager to 'drive up' standards in education, stating a desire for an educational system which promotes parity of access and opportunity. For example:

> Our schools should be engines of social mobility, helping children to overcome the accidents of birth and background to achieve much more than they may have ever imagined. But, at the moment, our schools system does not close gaps, it widens them. (Department for Education, 2010)

What is particularly notable in this quotation is the use of the phrase 'accidents of birth and background', as though people born in less-well-off families were somehow 'accidents' and that nothing can be done to change the situation. Perhaps then it is not surprising that UK governments have consistently, since the early 1990s, encouraged the use of 'ability' grouping. This is despite the overwhelming evidence that grouping pupils by 'ability' can in fact *promote* the very inequality policy-makers claim to be fighting. There is a belief (myth?) that grouping by 'ability' is indicative of rising standards and increased rigour, and it seems to be this that is reflected in the government's rhetoric. Becky Francis and her team (2016, p.7) have stressed that grouping pupils by 'ability' is made out by such governments to reflect British cultural values or '*natural* order', again suggesting that nothing can be done to change the situation. These cultural values have been sanctioned by the (elite) middle-classes who Francis et al. (p.10) described as the 'active consumers of education'. Partly because schools are keen to not only retain but also to attract middle-class families, schools have subsequently bought into the idea embedded within the government's narrative of 'ability' groups as being the natural way to proceed.

Jo Boaler and her team (2000) looked at the experiences of secondary school pupils studying mathematics in 'mixed ability' classes compared to classes divided into 'ability' sets. In research based on classroom observations and interviews with students, they found that 83 per cent of the students in the classes that were set (by 'ability') *wanted either to return to mixed 'ability' teaching or to change set*. Similarly, at primary school level, Dympna Devine (1993) explored pupils' experiences of within-class 'ability' grouping for reading. Most pupils indicated that they would least like to be in the lowest group (74 per cent) while 60 per cent wanted to be in the highest group because it gave them status and a feeling of superiority. During Devine's (1993) study, pupils seemed aware of the different kinds of teaching and activities that went on in different groups. Those in the 'highest' group were most satisfied with the activities that they undertook while 54 per cent of those in the lowest group expressed dissatisfaction with their activities. With the exception of those pupils in the 'top' reading groups, most pupils preferred whole-class or individual reading to group work because, as they explained, *these methods reduced feelings of being left out*.

Reay explained that too often 'ability' setting or grouping created a feeling of hopelessness in learners and undermined their sense of competence, autonomy *and relatedness to others*. The isolation that 'ability' grouping could foster tended to reinforce social class divisions. In other words, 'ability' grouping seemed to legitimise the differential treatment of pupils who tended to be, essentially, segregated according to social class (Gamoran et al., 1995). Additionally, where there was a lack of flexibility in movement between groups, an individual pupil's trajectory could often be determined at a very early age, even at Key Stage 1.

In terms of how pupils responded to these unfair opportunities, Jo Boaler (1997) suggested that pupils could experience feelings of anger and disappointment about what they believed to be unfair restrictions upon their potential: and consequently class stereotypes could be further played out. Adam Gamoran and colleagues (1995) found that behavioural expectations by teachers were anyway different for each group. They found that children in 'high ability' groups were allowed to disengage from learning in ways that still allowed them to complete a task, such as passing notes and making humorous remarks. They found that 'disruptive behaviour' was rare in 'higher' groups in comparison to 'lower' groups where pupils might refuse to participate. On occasions where behaviour between the two groups was similarly 'disruptive', these researchers found that teachers reacted differently to this behaviour in the high 'ability' groups.

Hallam and Parsons (2013) even suggested that the behaviour of pupils was overall more aggressive in schools where pupils were grouped by 'ability': they found that the more schools and teachers highlighted the differences between pupils in different groups, the more likely it became that incidents of negative behaviour would occur. This is in contrast to one of the key rationales given in favour of 'ability' grouping; that is, making it *easier* for the teacher to instruct pupils of different abilities.

Children's words: 'ability' grouping was okay for those at the top but even hard work did not get pupils into the top groups

Sean Macnamara, teacher-researcher and MA student (cited above), set out to consider the influences on pupils' learning of being relegated to 'low ability' groups. The 'low' groups were called *red* and *yellow groups* across all classes in his school from Reception to year 6 (ages 4–11). The 'top' group in all classes was *purple group*. Since Reception class, the children had been placed in these 'ability' groups. He talked to year 6 (aged 10–11) pupils about their experiences of being 'ability' grouped for all those years.

'Ability' grouping denoted social status in the classroom

The pupils Sean Macnamara interviewed seemed to believe that the purpose of school and of learning was simply to work hard in order to move up to the 'top ability' group and then try to stay there. In short, he found that 'ability' grouping influenced pupils quite dramatically, and thereby potentially interfered with their learning in a substantial way. This was primarily because the 'ability' group one belonged to was indicative of one's social status in their class where there appeared to be an atmosphere of social judgement. For example, Millie, a pupil in a middle 'ability' group, said that she felt 'frightened and very, very highly emotional' about the prospect of moving down a group:

> Because I know some of the children, they'll be rude to people in red and yellow [lowest 'ability' groups]. They'll say 'Oh, you got moved down'.

Pupil Alice spoke of being 'quite sad' about being in a lower 'ability' group and consequently being told by others 'Oh, you're so dumb'. Similarly, when asked whether he would feel concerned about being put in a low set when he started secondary school, Pupil Ben echoed his frustration with 'ability' groups by saying:

> ❝ I'd be unhappy and I wouldn't want to go to school. It would actually make me feel trapped. ❞

He added that he would also 'get really angry'. If he were moved up a group, on the other hand, he said that then he would feel encouraged and motivated to try harder. Indeed, pupils who were in 'more able' groups tended to be contented. Henry, who was in the 'top', purple group, actually 'felt really annoyed' at the imaginary idea of abolishing 'ability' groups and all pupils being placed into one 'mixed-ability' *purple* group, because he appeared to feel a sense of injustice at the idea. After all, *he had worked hard to get to the 'top' group*:

> ❝ I don't think it's right. Because they worked hard to be in purple group [the 'more able' group] if they already were [in purple group]: and now everyone else is. ❞

Peer-to-peer relationships seemed to be greatly affected by which 'ability' group a pupil was in, and the majority of pupils were worried about what their class-mates would say to them based upon which 'ability' group they were placed in. It was shockingly apparent that one could only be accepted as an equal member of the class, and only be respected, as a result of being in a 'more able' group. Curtis explained:

> ❝ I also felt kind of confused because – me and Yvonne, for example, we're work-ing all the time on our homework study on our table and no one really – *literally everyone ignored us*. But since we got up to purple and blue group [high ability groups], we were actually respected. We had some respect. ❞

Pupils sensed tension between the message that effort was important and being put in an 'ability' set

Despite the emotional impact that grouping pupils by 'ability' seemed to have, many pupils spoke of the importance that effort, trying and hard work had on being placed into different groups. Dan, a pupil working above national expectations, felt that the reason he was in the 'more able' (purple) group was because he was '*willing to try harder*' than other pupils. Ellen, another pupil in this group, agreed with Dan, telling Macnamara that they were both in 'top' groups because they had tried hard. Ellen appeared to value effort so much that she seemed unfazed at the prospect of moving down an 'ability' group because she told Macnamara: 'I can just try harder then I'll get back up.'

However, effort and hard work was not just an attribute that was valued by those pupils in the higher 'ability' groups but by many pupils. Millie, a pupil in a middle 'ability' group, believed effort to be very important and spoke about how her father always told her to 'try and try and try'. This seemed to affect Millie's mindset: when asked what the most important characteristic was for achievement, she said that it was definitely effort. However, perhaps most crucially, Millie also spoke of being discouraged and upset when despite her effort and willingness to 'try and try and try' she did not move up and stayed in an average 'ability' group. Pupil Millie said that her father 'was not very happy' about her lack of progress and this disturbed her. The importance of effort in order to be promoted seemed to be a message that many pupils were hearing from parents, revealing that parents were also affected by the status that 'ability' groups could project onto their child.

The importance of a growth mindset, the notion that 'ability' is not fixed (Dweck, 2006) and the idea that effort and hard work – not inbuilt 'ability' – are the core of learning, is an idea that many class teachers have been trying to promote in their classrooms. In a nutshell, as summarised by Chris Watkins, pupils with a fixed mindset (or a performance orientation) are concerned primarily about *proving* their competence while those with a growth mindset (or a learning orientation) are most concerned with *improving* their competence for the sake of that competence itself (see Chapter 3). Those with a fixed mindset are concerned to be seen as able in others' eyes and seek satisfaction from doing better than others, emphasising competition and public evaluation. Those with a growth mindset gain their satisfaction from succeeding in terms of their own goals (not prescribed by others), especially when these include tackling difficult tasks that they eventually master. The key difference is how 'success' is perceived: as proving to others that we can meet their requirements (whether through 'ability' or effort), or as recognising for oneself that improvement is being made because more challenging tasks are gradually being achieved.

It is disturbing, therefore, to see how pupils have married the ideas of having a growth mindset with being placed into 'ability' groups, trying to bring together two conflicting theories of learning. 'Ability' groups by definition imply a fixed mindset! It seems that the pupils understood 'ability' groups to be based upon the amount of effort they were willing to put in rather than the more widely accepted notion of an inbuilt academic 'ability'. However, while their progress continued to be measured using prescribed attainment criteria based on a hierarchical and fixed conception of knowledge, then 'growth' can only go in one restricted direction which can hardly be called 'growth' in a human sense at all. It is rather just repetitive practice towards a performance commissioned by someone else. If pupils believe that they are trying their best but still failing to make any progress against fixed assessment criteria, then pupils can feel all the more powerless and clearly 'trapped'.

For example, Millie described her upset when she thought that she had worked hard enough to move up to purple group (the 'more able' group):

❛ I remember in year 5 when Miss Ludlow made the big announcement of groups. I thought, 'This might be my chance to actually get into purple.' And I heard I was in green and I just got really upset. ❜

Demonstrating resilience and believing in effort, Millie went on to talk about how despite being upset, she was still motivated to try and move up groups:

❛ I went home, did some multiplication, some English, and then I felt confident the next day to get into purple. ❜

However, there was to be no happy ending for Millie whose efforts did not help her escape from the 'average' green group. Millie told Macnamara that she felt 'pretty sad because I really, really wanted to get into purple group.' What is clear is the confusion in Millie's mind between a growth mindset and the desire for external approval. She told Macnamara that she had done 'all that work for nothing!' – displaying the antipathy of a 'growth' mindset, despite her emphasis on effort rather than inert 'ability'.

Henry expressed similar discontentment regarding the groups he had been placed in:

> In year four I was in purple group for Maths and yellow group for English. [In] year five, I moved down to blue group for Maths.

Henry expressed his disappointment about moving down in Maths:

> Because I thought I was okay but it turned out I wasn't. I tried my hardest and now I just had to move down.

Henry felt that he had 'failed a little bit'. He had been hoping for external recognition and none had been forthcoming, *despite his continued hard work and effort*.

Pressure was imposed by 'ability' grouping and the associated comparisons across pupils

In keeping with their desire to improve their status in the classroom, the majority of pupils reported that they felt under pressure at some point during school as a consequence of being in 'ability' groups. Curtis admitted to being so worried about which group he was in that he would be 'secretive' about it at home. He seemed to fear his family's anger at his lack of success, who saw 'high ability' groups as indicators of success:

> [B]asically I was moved down and I was barely talking to my parents or my sisters.

Contrastingly, pupil Simon reflected how he was able to work at his own pace without having to worry about this pressure because his parents did not have external goals for him to reach:

> Some parents, they want their kids to get a good grade and go to Grammar School and stuff so they can go to a private school. But my mum's not pressuring me on that, so I can just work to my ability.

However, Simon did still make reference to peer pressure:

> When I was in year 5, most people like put pressure on you if you get something wrong. Like that person got like 48 on their tests and you got like 15, they'll keep saying, 'Oh my Gosh! I got 48, I got 48 and you got lower than me!'.

Peer pressure and pupils comparing one another's 'ability' seemed to be a theme that many pupils raised, again suggesting a social atmosphere laden with judgement in their classroom. There was one comment of critique about this situation which came from pupil Ellen, who seemed to have a learning orientation as well as a sense of compassion:

> Because if someone's struggling, instead of bragging about being smarter than them, they should help them.

However, in general, pressure from home or pressure from peers through name calling and comparison appears to have had a negative impact on pupils' well-being and their attitudes to learning. A sense of helplessness was demonstrated in the face of fearing others' judgements. 'Ability' groups fed into this atmosphere of social judgement and comparison which even those in the 'top' groups feared.

How 'ability' grouping stigmatised help-seeking

In an atmosphere of social judgement, pupils came to value working and learning without help from their class-mates because their peers could be seen as competitors rather than support-givers. The pupils additionally appeared to view negatively situations where support was needed from the class teacher or another adult too. Admitting to needing help might be construed as needing to move down a group. Thus help-seeking, an essential aspect of autonomous learning, was considered only appropriate for those in the red ('bottom') group. As Ray explained:

> Well, you've got red group, which is the lowest ability, which means that they need like a bit of help. Because you'll have the people who don't really understand the work. And then you've got the purple group, which is they don't really need help: they're capable of doing it by their self.

Thus, interaction and collaboration among pupils and between pupils and the teacher was neglected as a tool for growth among those of 'higher ability'.

Summary of the influences of 'ability' grouping
in this primary classroom

In summary, Sean Macnamara's small-scale research revealed some valuable insights about children's experiences of classrooms from the point of view of 'ability' grouping, which often equates with social class grouping too. Although the pupils all seemed to believe that their grouping was based on effort rather than inert 'ability', it transpired that they believed that some children *could* make more effort than others, and that it was these children who deserved the high status of being in the 'top ability' groups. Because these children could make more effort, they gained higher status in the classroom. Effort here has become *conflated* with inert 'ability' instead of being seen as a means to *improve* competence rather than to *prove* it. In addition, by one child proving their competence and arriving at purple group, others are meanwhile more tempted to give up since for them, effort clearly does not work in the race to the top of the performance league. They come to see themselves as the less authoritative in the class.

The children who did have the 'ability' to expend more effort (as the children perceived it) reached the top reward of being in purple group and had high status among peers and teachers alike. However, this did not mean they were engaging in learning in a more sophisticated way than the peers they competed against. One can even imagine that in purple group, children might rest on their laurels rather than tackle ever more sophisticated challenges, especially as they were afraid to ask for help from others. Meanwhile, children in 'lower' groups would certainly follow standard rather than creative routes to 'success' (i.e. being in purple group), given its importance to how respected and valued they felt. Because this 'success' was actually not attainable by most children in the classroom, this fed into an atmosphere of social judgement and comparison rather than one of collaboration and interaction. The children in the 'top ability' groups might feel good about themselves, but this was perhaps at the expense of enriching their own learning. The children in the other groups also had no space to enrich their own learning as they fought with tunnel vision to reach the 'top'.

Schiro's first purpose for schooling and its relationship to cultural capital as played out in the classroom

Lisa Nandy (2012) suggested that to be fair to all children

> the system must equip them for life, not just the workforce and allow school to be a place where they find social enlightenment, not social advantage. (p.677)

In terms of Schiro's four ideologies for public education, if 'the purpose of education is to help children learn the accumulated knowledge of our culture: that of the academic disciplines', the research studies described in the pages above would suggest that so far classrooms are not achieving their goal among all young people, and perhaps it would suggest that this goal is inappropriate for the working life offered to some young people today. Andy Green (1990) singled out England as the most explicit example of a schooling system that applied Schiro's first philosophy of public education in order that the dominant class (i.e. the powerful, middle-class) secured hegemony over subordinate groups (i.e. such as the working-classes).

Alice Sullivan and colleagues (2014) have described how Bourdieu and Passeron's notion of *cultural* capital may be helpful in explaining education's role in creating and reproducing social divisions and economic inequalities. For Bourdieu and Passeron ([1977] 1990), cultural rather than economic resources were fundamental to determining educational inequalities. The paradox is that the institution in government that is most meritocratic, the education system, is also the institution that is most complicit in the reproduction of social inequality. Bernstein (1977, 1995), through his work on restricted and elaborated codes, suggested that cultural capital overrode any levelling tendencies public education systems may have had, through the way that *cultural codes* operated. Bernstein noted that it would take years, if not generations, to accumulate and then to dissolve these cultural codes. Of particular note regarding these notions is the fact that the accumulated advantages among the elite groups are *disguised*.

Bourdieu's interpretation of cultural capital is not seen as consisting in 'beaux arts' elite cultural activities such as visiting the opera or art exhibitions, but as including knowledge and skills which are *rewarded within an education system that embodies the transmission of cultural heritage* as suggested by Schiro's first purpose for state-funded schooling. Previous studies have found that newspapers and books in the home and reading behaviour rather than 'beaux arts' participation help to explain social differentials in children's education. Reading, and linked to this, writing, may be distinctive because it develops linguistic skills at the same time as wider cultural knowledge (Sullivan, 2002, 2007).

The *normalising* tendency in authoritarian regimes, including classrooms, has also been theorised by Bourdieu (1990; see Chapter 2). He employed the term 'linguistic domination' to illustrate the powerful party's (i.e. the middle-class teacher's) capacity for creating a unity through the use of an official, legitimated and normalised language, against which all forms of linguistic and other practices were measured, thereby dispossessing and marginalising the least dominant classes. Oppression in this sense was hidden not only in but also behind discourse through the conventions related to language, which excluded some discourses and favoured the dominant ones in the interest of one particular group of people (Fairclough, 2000).

Alice Sullivan and her colleagues (2014) among others have defended the usefulness of distinguishing between cultural resources on the one hand and economic resources on the other. Sullivan and colleagues noted the important distinction made by Boudon (1974) between the 'primary' and 'secondary' effects of social divisions. The 'primary effects' of stratification were defined as cultural inequalities that determined the academic attainment of pupils. Boudon suggested: 'The lower the social status, the poorer the cultural background – hence the lower the school achievement' (p.29).

The 'secondary effects' of stratification were, according to Boudon, due to the costs and benefits associated with different educational decisions for students from different social classes. These educational decisions occurred at key transition points, such as the move from secondary to post-secondary education. According to Boudon, the secondary effects of social stratification were due not only to cultural inequalities but also to economic inequalities. It was claimed that the 'secondary effects' of social stratification were more important than the primary effects because they were exponential, *with each subsequent transition in the education system increasing the level of inequality*. Interestingly, recent research has shown that ethnic minority status worked in the opposite direction to classic 'secondary effects' in Britain, leading to increased participation by minorities at any given level of schooling.

Schiro's further purposes for schooling: have these been met in relation to working-class pupils?

Advocates of the 'social efficiency ideology' who see the purpose of schooling to be 'efficiently meet[ing] the needs of society by training youth to function as future mature contributing members of society' might also be disappointed in the outcomes from classrooms currently (Schiro, 2013, p.5). The research findings above suggest that 'youth' as a whole unit do not all contribute maturely to satisfying the needs of society. Indeed, as part of society, their needs are not always being met and nor are they meeting the needs of society. In this ideology, classroom learning is about learning skills which will be useful for future employment, such as employability, flexibility, collaborative skills; but clearly there is a current mismatch between what is learnt in classrooms and adequate employment opportunities, most particularly for working-class pupils.

In Schiro's (2013, pp.5–6) 'learner-centred' ideology, 'the goal of education is the growth of individuals: his or her own unique intellectual, social, emotional and physical attributes.' In classrooms which entertain the learner-centred ideology, the pupil's everyday cognitive, affective, social and physical development and flourishing are the means and the ends of classroom learning. The research above, and indeed this whole book, suggests that as a philosophy, this approach is yet to be fulfilled. Many pupils do not experience intellectual, social or emotional growth as a key aspect of schooling. Even schools effective in enhancing middle-class attainment are not necessarily effective in enhancing the social or emotional well-being of their pupils.

The 'social reconstruction ideology' suggests that the purpose of education is the development of a 'critically educated citizenry able to engage reflectively and reflexively with the wider society, opening up greater possibilities for radical societal change' (p.6). Radical societal change, including greater social mobility and greater equality, are goals whose fulfilment currently seems to be retreating rather than being more nearly met. Part of the reason for listening to children's voices from classrooms through this book is so that all children can better engage critically, reflectively and reflexively with the wider society. This is the ideology that requires most transformation of the classroom as we know it today.

Children's words: transformation occurred through the reading and writing of the Freedom Writers

A young, just-qualified teacher in South Beach, California chose to take her first teaching job in a school that had just undergone 'integration'. In other words, this school had just become a comprehensive school in the sense that students of any race and any 'ability' could now attend this highly successful institution. This was an attractive option for underprivileged students from deprived areas where there existed no good schools. Students were therefore bussed in from long distances away, increasing the range of ethnicities and cultures represented in the school. The young teacher, Erin Gruwell, dubbed by her students as 'Miss G', had hopes of improving social justice through her teaching. She found herself teaching English to multi-cultural classes of students whose schooling was considered by other teachers in the school as a *waste of time* because the teachers assumed that those [working-class, multi-ethnic] students could not or would not learn.

Miss G's head teacher told her:

> You can't make someone want an education ... you can only make them obey.

Miss G's husband told her:

> No talented teacher should waste their talents on people who don't give a damn about education.

The 2007 film entitled *The Freedom Writers* illustrated the true story of Miss G as she struggled to support these disaffected, impoverished students and indeed, give them opportunities to excel. She discovered through frustration that traditional teaching methods and curricula did not help these students to learn. She realised that before any formal learning could happen, she needed to understand her students' experiences of the classroom and the teacher, as she could sense the rift between her own and her students' perceptions and feelings. These are some of the students' words that she had not expected:

> Teachers don't make substantial changes to students' lives.
>
> Teachers have to earn respect.
>
> Teachers don't know the pain students feel.

By interacting with these students, she perceived that failure to learn was mainly to do with their lack of relatedness to school and to wider society where they did not feel they had a valuable voice or a respected role to play. Miss G defied all the negative voices in her environment to demonstrate that teaching was not just about being an expert in her subject but that each teacher also needed to be emotionally and socially sensitive. After several months, one student described Miss G's classroom as:

> The only place where students really get to be themselves.

Noticing that gang warfare dominated their difficult lives, Miss G engaged her class in everyday literature about gangs, gradually moving into *The Diary of Anne Frank*, victim of the worst gang in history (as she put it) – the Nazis. By focusing on the racial violence faced by all her students and by relating it to racial violence in history and in current affairs, she helped her impoverished class to talk and write about their own experiences. While her endeavours dramatically improved their reading and writing skills, equally important was the fact that they allowed the pupils to start to express their pain; to relate this to the suffering of others; to develop a sense of their own identities; and then to act differently.

It is a heart-warming story of transformational learning in which the destructive assumptions about students from the most disadvantaged social backgrounds were radically challenged. They gradually came to realise that they had the power to influence the procedures and practices which shaped not only their learning but also their disadvantaged lives. Many of these students, instead of being shot by the time they were 16, ultimately graduated from universities. The sense of self, of autonomy, of their own authority, that Miss G inspired in these students allowed them to *see themselves in a different way* and therefore to act differently in and on the world.

Valuing pupils for what they are: transformation at St George-in-the-East secondary modern school

Michael Fielding wrote about another inspiring teacher, head teacher Alex Bloom. He opened St George-in-the-East secondary modern school, in Stepney, London on 1 October 1945 'with some 260 boys and girls from neighbouring schools', most of whom came from impoverished working-class backgrounds (Fielding, 2005, p.2). In those days, schools in England were explicitly segregated by attainment, which mainly equated with social class. Secondary modern schools were for the least-high attainers who failed their 11+ exam, while Grammar Schools were for high attainers. Today most state-funded schools are segregated less explicitly, being nominally 'comprehensive'. In reality, the segregation lives on but within the school, with 'ability' setting and streaming within year groups replacing segregated schools, as exemplified so well in Sean Macnamara's classroom (above).

Bloom decided that if his radical vision of education was to stand any chance of succeeding, he needed to start with the basics and build 'a truly democratic community' where all pupils felt a sense of competence, autonomy and relatedness, regardless of class, race, gender or recorded attainment. He recognised that this would mean completely disbanding the vestiges of authoritarian approaches: 'A consciously democratic community could not be formed gradually by the removal of one taboo after another.' Thus, the school 'began without regimentation, without corporal punishment, without competition'. Fielding (2005) wrote of Bloom:

His fundamental starting point was our humanity, our being and development as persons. Our sense of who we are, our worth and capacity to feel and be significant go hand in hand with our capacity to contribute to the community within which our sense of significance and uniqueness grows and flourishes. In Bloom's experience, St George-in-the-East's children emerging from primary schools invariably felt 'inferior' and 'unwanted'. His response was to provide a school community that took an entirely different view of them; one which believed that 'What the child is was much more important than what the child could do'; one that sought to replace the debilitating influence of fear as the prime incentive to 'progress'. 'Fear of authority (... imposed for disciplinary purposes), fear of failure (... by means of marks, prizes and competition); and the fear of punishment (for all these purposes)' must be replaced by 'friendship, security and the recognition of each child's worth'. (p.3)

Fielding noted how two of the most important driving forces of the 'school pattern' at this radical school were that the child 'must feel that s/he does count, that s/he is wanted, that s/he has a contribution to make to the common good' (Fielding, 2005, p.3). And as Bloom noted, the child had to feel that the school community was itself actually worthwhile in order that community and individuality interacted in a virtuous upward spiral, whereby pupils willingly gave their consent to engage both in learning and with the community. Bloom emphasised two other fundamentals: first, that any form of competition other than against oneself was not acceptable. The only prize that was allowed was the 'prizing' of every student (Rogers, 1957, p.5). Second, that students exercised as a matter of course the capacity to make choices about what, how, when and with whom they learnt. They were thereby treated as competent and maturely responsible people who had the power to influence the procedures and practices which shaped their learning and ultimately their lives. The barriers created by 'ability' grouping and by social class segregation could be dealt with in alternative ways which emphasised – rather than diminished – the pupil's own sense of authority.

ACTIVITIES FOR TEACHERS: SOME PRACTICAL WAYS FORWARD FOR TEACHERS AND OTHER EDUCATORS IN THE CLASSROOM

Discussion or journal writing

With a partner or in a private learning journal, describe one working-class child you have known and/or taught. What were they like? Did they fit your expectations of 'working-class'? If so, in which ways?

To what extent are children in the classrooms you know aware of social class and the reasons for inequality in society? How much focus do you give issues of social justice in the classroom?

What can be learned from the above examples in Chapter 5 for classroom practice with children? In particular, consider:

- Social segregation within the classroom.

- Teachers' views of working-class pupils.

- Links between 'ability' grouping and social class.

- Approaches to lessening the gap between social classes in the classroom.

- What examples of transformational teachers can you yourself cite?

Actions to try out

Try asking pupils to tell each other about and to record for the teacher their experiences of feeling 'different' when in a group. How did it feel? How did it make the child act? What could the group have done differently to support this child more?

(Continued)

(Continued)

What happens when the teacher deliberately notes down which students are from working-class backgrounds? Do they show any common characteristics? Do you show any common ways of relating to this group?

Keep a tally of how often you consult middle-class children compared to working-class children.

Plenary

Describe, reflect on and analyse for yourself or in a pair/group, what happened when these actions were tried out in classrooms.

How could you engage children in evaluating the actions you tried out?

References

Affouneh, S. and Hargreaves, E. (2015). Fear in the Palestinian Classroom: Pedagogy, Authoritarianism and Transformation. *Pedagogies: An International Journal*, 10 (3), pp. 222–37.

Armstrong, D. (2006). *Experiences of special education*. London: RoutledgeFalmer.

Assor, A. (2012). Allowing Choice and Nurturing an Inner Compass: Educational Practices Supporting Students' Need for Autonomy. In: S. Christenson, A. Reschly, and C. Wylie, eds, *Handbook of research on student engagement*. New York: Springer. pp. 421–39.

Barbeau, E., Krieger, N. and Soobader, M. (2004). Working Class Matters: Socioeconomic Disadvantage, Race/Ethnicity, Gender and Smoking in NHIS 2000. *American Journal of Public Health*, 94 (2), pp. 269–78.

Bernstein, B. (1971). On the Classification and Framing of Educational Knowledge. In: M.F.D. Young, ed., *Knowledge and control*. London: Collier Macmillan, pp. 47–69.

Bernstein, B. (1977). *Class, codes and control, Vol. 3*. London: Routledge.

Bernstein, B. (1995). *Pedagogy, symbolic control and identity*. London: Taylor & Francis.

Black, P. and Wiliam, D. (2006). *Inside the black box: raising standards through classroom assessment*. London: Granada Learning.

Boaler, J. (1997). Setting, Social Class and Survival of the Quickest. *British Educational Research Journal*, 23 (5), pp. 575–95.

Boaler, J., Wiliam, D. and Brown, M. (2000). Experiences of Ability Grouping – Disaffection, Polarization and the Construction of Failure. *British Educational Research Journal*, 28 (5), pp. 631–48.

Boudon, R. (1974). *Education, opportunity, and social inequality: changing prospects in western society*. New York: Wiley.

Bourdieu, P. (1990). *The logic of practice*. Cambridge: Polity Press.

Bourdieu, P. and Passeron, J-C. ([1977] 1990). *Reproduction in education, society and culture*. London/Beverly Hills: Sage.

Brown, A.L., Ash, D., Rutherford, M., Nakagawa, K., Gordon, A. and Campione, J.C. (1993). Distributed Expertise in the Classroom. In: G. Salomon, ed., *Distributed cognitions: psychological and educational considerations*. Cambridge: CUP, pp. 188–228.

Burke, C. and Grosvenor, I. (2003). *The school I'd like*. London: RoutledgeFalmer.

Campbell, T. (2014). Stratified at Seven: In-Class Ability Grouping and the Relative Affect. *British Educational Research Journal*, 40 (5), pp. 749–71.

Caron, C. (2014). Book review: Raby, Rebecca, 'School Rules: Obedience, Discipline, and Elusive Democracy'. *Canadian Journal of Sociology*, 39 (2), pp. 303–6.

Crossouard, B. (2011). Using Formative Assessment to Support Complex Learning in Conditions of Social Adversity. *Assessment in Education: Principles, Policy & Practice*, 18 (1), pp. 59–72.

Deci, E.L., Schwartz, A.J, Sheinman, L. and Ryan, R.M. (1981). An Instrument to Assess Adults' Orientations Toward Control Versus Autonomy with Children: Reflections on Intrinsic Motivation and Perceived Competence. *Journal of Educational Psychology*, 73 (5), pp. 642–50.

Department of Education (2010). *The importance of teaching – the schools White Paper 2010*. Available at: www.gov.uk/government/uploads/system/uploads/attachment_data/file/ 175429/CM-7980.pdf (accessed 21 Dec. 2015).

Devine, D. (1993). A Study of Reading Ability Groups: Primary School Children's Experiences and Views. *Irish Educational Studies*, 12(1), pp. 134–42.

Devine, D. (2003). *Children, power and schooling: how childhood is structured in the primary school*. Sterling, VA: Stylus Publishing.

Devine, D. and McGillicuddy, D. (2016). Positioning Pedagogy – A Matter of Human Rights. *Oxford Review of Education*, 42 (4), pp. 424–43.

Dewey, J. (1899). *The school and society and the child and the curriculum*. Overland Park, KS: Digireads.com Publishing.

Dewey, J. (1938). *Education and experience*. New York: Simon and Schuster.

Dewey, J. (2011). *Democracy and education*. Milton Keynes: Simon Brown.

Dunne, M. and Gazeley, L. (2008). Teachers, Social Class and Underachievement. *British Journal of Sociology of Education*, 29 (5), pp. 451–63.

Dweck, C.S. (2006). *Mindset: the new psychology of success*. London: Robinson.

Edwards, A. (2005). Let's Get Beyond Community and Practice: The Many Meanings of Learning by Constructing or Co-constructing Knowledge. *Curriculum Journal*, 16 (1), pp. 49–66.

Fairclough, N. (2000). *New labour, new language?* London: Psychology Press.

Fielding, M. (1996). Beyond Collaboration: On the Importance of Community. In: D. Bridges and C. Husbands, eds, *Consorting & collaborating in the education market place*. London: RoutledgeFalmer, pp. 149–67.

Fielding, M. (2004). Transformative Approaches to Student Voice: Theoretical Underpinnings, Recalcitrant Realities. *British Research Journal*, 30 (2), pp. 295–311.

Fielding, M. (2005). Alex Bloom, Pioneer of Radical State Education. *Forum For Promoting 3-19 Comprehensive Education*, 47 (2/3), pp. 1–15.

Filer, J. (2014). *Does choice support learning?* MA dissertation, UCL Institute of Education.

Fisher, H. (2011). Inside the Primary Classroom: Examples of Dissatisfaction Behind a Veil of Compliance. *British Journal of Educational Studies*, 59 (2), pp. 121–41.

Flink, C., Boggiano, A.K. and Barrett, M. (1990). Controlling Teaching Strategies: Undermining Children's Self-Determination and Performance. *Journal of Personality and Social Psychology*, 59 (5), pp. 916–24.

Foucault, M. (1978). *Discipline and Punish: The Birth of the Prison*. New York: Random House.

Francis, B. and Mills, M. (2012). Schools as Damaging Organisations: Instigating a Dialogue Concerning Alternative Models of Schooling. *Pedagogy, Culture and Society*, 20 (2), pp. 251–71.

Francis, B., Archer, L., Hodgen, J., Pepper, D., Taylor, B. and Travers, M. (2016). Exploring the Relative Lack of Impact of Research on 'Ability Grouping' in England: a Discourse Analytic Account. *Cambridge Journal of Education*, January, pp. 1–17.

Freire, P. (1972). *Pedagogy of the oppressed*. London: Penguin.

Freire, P. (1998). *Pedagogy of freedom: ethics, democracy and civic courage*. Lanham, MD: Rowman & Littlefield.

Gamoran, A., Nystrand, M., Berends, M. and LePore, P.C. (1995). An Organizational Analysis of the Effects of Ability Grouping. *American Educational Research Journal*, 32, pp. 687–715.

Gause, C. (2011). *Diversity, equity, and inclusive education: a voice from the margins.* Dordrecht: Sense Publishers.

Gillborn, D. and Youdell, D. (2000). *Rationing education.* Buckingham: Open University Press.

Gipps, C., Hargreaves, E. and McCallum, B. (2015). *What makes a good primary school teacher?: Expert classroom strategies.* London: Routledge.

Giroux, H. (2005). *Against the new authoritarianism: politics after Abu Gharib.* Winnipeg: Arbiter Ring.

Gratton, R. (2012). *The 'reality' of learning as, with and because of a 'collaborative learning group'.* MA dissertation, UCL Institute of Education.

Green, A. (1990). *Education and state formation: the rise of education systems in England, France and the U.S.A.* London: Palgrave Macmillan.

Green, F., Machin, S., Murphy, R. and Zhu, Y. (2012). The Changing Economic Advantage from Private Schools. *Economica*, 79 (316), pp. 658–79.

Gruwell, E. (2007). *The freedom writers diary.* New York: Broadway Books.

Hallam, S. and Parsons, S. (2013). Prevalence of Streaming in UK Primary Schools: Evidence from the Millennium Cohort Study. *British Educational Research Journal*, 39 (3), pp. 514–44.

Harber, C. (2015). Violence in Schools: The Role of Authoritarian Learning. In: D. Scott and E. Hargreaves, ed., *The SAGE handbook of learning.* London: Sage, pp. 243–53.

Hargreaves, E. (2011). Teachers' Feedback to Pupils: 'Like So Many Bottles Thrown Out to Sea?'. In: R. Berry and B. Anderson, eds, *Assessment reform in education.* London: Springer, pp. 121–34.

Hargreaves, E. (2012). Teacher's Classroom Feedback: Still Trying to Get It Right. *Pedagogies: An International Journal*, 7 (1), pp. 1–15.

Hargreaves, E. (2013). Inquiring into Children's Experiences of Teacher Feedback: Reconceptualising Assessment for Learning. *Oxford Review of Education*, 39 (2), pp. 229–46.

Hargreaves, E. (2014). The Practice of Promoting Primary Pupils' Autonomy: Examples of Teacher Feedback. *Educational Research*, 56 (3), pp. 295–309.

Hargreaves, E. (2015). 'I Think it Helps You Better When You're Not Scared': Fear and Learning in the Primary Classroom. *Pedagogy, Culture and Society*, 23 (4), pp. 617–38.

Hargreaves, E. and Affouneh, S. (2017). Pupils' Fear in the Classroom: Portraits from Palestine and England. *Journal of Research in Childhood Education: An International Journal of Research on the Education of Children*, doi:10.1080/02568543.2016.127 2508.

Hargreaves, E., Mahgoub, M. and Elhawary, D. (2016). *An investigation into improved primary school English learning in the crowded classroom: pupils explain what teachers and children can do to make progress (An Egyptian case study).* British Council. Online report available at www.teachingenglish.org.uk/sites/teacheng/files/G164%20ELTRA%20An%20investigation%20into%20improved%20primary%20school%20FINAL_WEB.pdf (accessed 21 Feb. 2017).

Hattie, J. and Timperley, H. (2007). The Power of Feedback. *Review of Educational Research*, 77 (1), pp. 81–112.

Henderlong, J. and Lepper, M.R. (2002). The Effects of Praise on Children's Intrinsic Motivation: A Review and Synthesis. *Psychological Bulletin*, 128 (5), p. 774.

Holliday, A. (1994). *Appropriate methodology and social context.* Cambridge: Cambridge University Press.

Holt, J. (1964). *How children fail.* West Drayton: Penguin.

Hopkins, E. (2008). Classroom Conditions to Secure Enjoyment and Achievement: The Pupils' Voice. *Listening to the Voice of Every Child Matters*, 36 (4), pp. 393–401.

Illeris, K. (2007). *How we learn: learning and non-learning in school and beyond.* London: Routledge.

Jackson, C. (2010). Fear in Education. *Educational Review*, 62 (1), pp. 39–52.

James, M. (2006). Assessment, Teaching and Theories of Learning. In: J. Gardner, ed., *Assessment and learning.* London: Sage, pp. 47–60.

James, M. (2011). Assessment for Learning: Research and Policy in the (Dis)United Kingdom. In: R. Berry and D. Adamson, eds, *Assessment reform in education.* London: Springer, pp. 15–32.

Jones, O. (2011). *Chavs: the demonization of the working class.* London: Verso.

Katz, I. and Assor, A. (2007). When Choice Motivates and When it Does Not. *Educational Psychology Review*, 19, pp. 429–42.

Keep, E. (2009). Internal and External Incentives to Engage in Education and Training – a Framework for Analysing the Forces Acting on Individuals. *SKOPE Monograph*, 19.

Kemmis, S. (2006). Participatory Action Research and the Public Sphere. *Education Action Research*, 14 (4), pp. 459–76.

Kohn, A. (1996). *Beyond discipline.* Alexandria, VA: Association for Supervision and Curriculum Development.

Lefstein, A. (2002). Thinking Power and Pedagogy Apart: Coping with Discipline in Progressivist School Reform. *Teachers College Record*, 104 (8), pp. 1627–55.

Lemke, T., Thorup Larsen, L. and Hvibbak, T. (2011). Fear. *Distinktion: Scandinavian Journal of Social Theory*, 12 (2), pp. 113–14.

Lin, A.M. (2007). What's the Use of 'Triadic Dialogue?': Activity Theory, Conversation Analysis, and Analysis of Pedagogical Practices. *Pedagogies: An International Journal*, 2 (2), pp. 77–94.

Little, D. (1991). *Autonomy: definitions, issues and problems.* Dublin: Authentik.

MacInnes, T., Aldridge, H., Bushe, S., Kenway, P. and Tinson, A. (2013). *Monitoring poverty and social exclusion 2013.* York: Joseph Rowntree Foundation and The New Policy Institute. Online report available at www.jrf.org.uk/report/monitoring-poverty-and-social-exclusion-2013 (accessed 29 Sept. 2016).

MacInnes, T., Aldridge, H., Parekh, A. and Kenway, P. (2012). *Monitoring poverty and social exclusion in Northern Ireland 2012.* York: Joseph Rowntree Foundation. Online report available at www.jrf.org.uk/report/monitoring-poverty-and-social-exclusion-northern-ireland-2012 (accessed 29 Sept. 2016).

MacIntyre, D., Peddar, D. and Ruddock, J. (2005). Pupil Voice: Comfortable and Uncomfortable Learnings for Teachers. *Research Papers in Education*, 20 (2), pp. 149–68.

Macleod, G., MacAllister, J. and Pirrie, A. (2012). Towards a Broader Understanding of Authority in Student-Teacher Relationships. *Oxford Review of Education*, 38 (4), pp. 493–508.

Marmot, M. (2004). Status Syndrome: How Your Social Standing Directly Affects Your Health and Life Expectancy. *Significance*, 1 (4), pp. 150–54.

Marton, F. and Booth, S.A. (1997). *Learning and awareness.* Hove: Psychology Press.

McCallum, B., Hargreaves, E. and Gipps, C. (2000). Learning: The Pupil's Voice. *Cambridge Journal of Education*, 30 (2), pp. 275–389.

Meighan, R. and Harber, C. (2007). *A sociology of educating.* New York: Continuum.

Mesirow, J. (2006). An Overview of Transformative Learning. In: P. Sutherland and J. Crowther, eds, *Lifelong learning: concepts and contexts.* Abingdon: Routledge, pp. 24–38.

Miller, A. (1983) *For your own good: hidden cruelty in child rearing and the roots of violence.* New York: Noonday Press.

Ministry of Education, F-Grupacija, Macedonia (2016). *Analysis of the current situation in the Republic of Macedonia and the characteristics of the educational system in the secondary education.* Skopje: Ministry of Education.

Miskin, R. (2006a). *Read write inc. phonics: phonics handbook*. Oxford: Oxford University Press.

Miskin, R. (2006b). *Read write inc. phonics: speed sounds lesson plans*. Oxford: Oxford University Press.

Moore, A. (2013). Love and Fear in the Classroom: How 'Validating Affect' Might Help us Understand Young Students and Improve Their Experiences of School Life and Learning. In: M. O'Loughlin, ed., *The uses of psychoanalysis in working with children's emotional lives*. Lanham, MD: Jason Aronson, pp. 285–304.

Moore, A. (2015). Knowledge, Curriculum and Learning: 'What Did You Learn in School?'. In: D. Scott and E. Hargreaves, eds, *The SAGE handbook of learning*. London: Sage, pp. 144–54.

Nandy, L. (2012). What Would a Socially Just Education System Look Like? *Journal of Education Policy*, 27 (5), pp. 677–80.

Nash, P. (1966). *Authority and freedom in education*. New York: Wiley.

Nassaji, H. and Wells, G. (2000). What's the Use of 'Triadic Dialogue'?: An Investigation of Teacher-Student Interaction. *Applied Linguistics*, 21, pp. 376–406.

Nicol, D.J. and Macfarlane-Dick, D. (2006). Formative Assessment and Self-Regulated Learning: A Model and Seven Principles of Good Feedback Practice. *Studies in Higher Education*, 31 (2), pp. 199–218.

Niemi, R., Kumpulainen, K., Lipponen, L. and Hilppö, J. (2015). Pupils' Perspectives on the Lived Pedagogy of the Classroom. *Education 3-13: International Journal of Primary, Elementary and Early Years Education*, 43 (6), pp. 683–99.

Noddings, N. (2005). Identifying and Responding to Needs in Education. *Cambridge Journal of Education*, 35(2), pp. 147–59.

Nordlander, E., Strandh, M. and Brännlund, A. (2015). What Does Class Origin and Education Mean for the Capabilities of Agency and Voice? *British Journal of Sociology of Education*, 36 (2), pp. 291–312.

OECD (2010). *The education at a glance report from the OECD*. Paris: OECD.

Opdenakker, M. and Van Damme, J. (2000). Effects of Schools, Teaching Staff and Classes on Achievement and Well-Being in Secondary Education: Similarities and Differences Between School Outcomes. *School Effectiveness and School Improvement*, 11 (2), pp. 165–96.

Pace, J. and Hemmings, A. (2006). *Classroom authority*. Mahwah, NJ: Lawrence Erlbaum.

Patall, E. (2012). The Motivational Complexity of Choosing: A Review of Theory and Research. In: R. Ryan, ed., *The Oxford handbook of human motivation*. New York: Oxford University Press, pp. 248–79.

Patall, E., Cooper, H. and Robinson, J. (2008). The Effects of Choice on Intrinsic Motivation and Related Outcomes: A Meta-analysis of Research Findings. *Psychological Bulletin*, 134 (2), pp. 270–300.

Perrenoud, P. (1998). From Formative Evaluation to a Controlled Regulation of Learning Towards a Wider Conceptual Field. *Assessment in Education*, 5, pp. 85–102.

Piaget, J. (1925). Psychologie et Critique de la Connaissance. *Archives de Psychologie*, 29 (75), 193–210.

Pratt, N. (2007). *Democracy and authoritarianism in the Arab world*. London: Lynne Rienner.

Pryor, J. and Crossouard, B. (2008). A Socio-Cultural Theorisation of Formative Assessment. *Oxford Review of Education*, 34, pp. 1–20.

Quick, L. (2015). 'Tricks': pupil perspectives of non-compliance in the primary classroom. MA dissertation, UCL Institute of Education.

Raby, R. (2012). *School rules: obedience, discipline, and elusive democracy*. Toronto: University of Toronto Press.

Reay, D. (1995). 'They Employ Cleaners to Do That': Habitus in the Primary Classroom. *British Journal of Sociology of Education*, 36 (2), pp. 353–71.

Reay, D. (2005). Beyond Consciousness? The Psychic Landscape of Social Class. *Sociology*, 39 (5), pp. 911–28.

Reay, D. (2006). The Zombie Stalking English Schools: Social Class and Educational Inequality. *British Journal of Educational Studies*, 54 (3), pp. 288–307.

Reay, D. (2012). What Would a Socially Just Education System Look Like?: Saving the Minnows from the Pike. *Journal of Education Policy*, 27 (5), pp. 587–99.

Rogalsky, J. (2009). 'Mythbusters': Dispelling the Culture of Poverty Myth in the Urban Classroom. *Journal of Geography*, 108 (4–5), pp. 198–209.

Rogers, C.R. (1957). The Necessary and Sufficient Conditions of Therapeutic Personality Change. *Journal of Consulting Psychology*, 21 (2), pp. 95.

Romanish, B. (1995). Authority, Authoritarianism, and Education. *Education and Culture*, XII (2), pp. 17–25.

Rudduck, J. and Fielding, M. (2006). Student Voice and the Perils of Popularity. *Educational Review*, 58 (2), pp. 219–31.

Ryan, R.M. and Deci, E.L. (2000). Self-Determination Theory and the Facilitation of Intrinsic Motivation, Social Development, and Well-Being. *American Psychologist*, 55 (1), pp. 68.

Sadler, D.R. (1989). Formative Assessment and the Design of Instructional Systems. *Instructional Science*, 18 (2), pp. 119–44.

Saevi, T. (2015). Learning and Pedagogic Relations. In: D. Scott and E. Hargreaves, eds, *The SAGE handbook of learning*. London: Sage, pp. 342–52.

Schiro, M. (2013). *Curriculum theory: conflicting visions and enduring concerns*. Thousand Oaks, CA: Sage.

Shepard, L.A. (2000). The Role of Assessment in a Learning Culture. *Educational Researcher*, 29 (7), pp. 4–14.

Skidmore, C., Cuff, N. and Leslie, C. (2007). *Invisible children*. London: The Bow Group.

Southgate, E. (2003). *Remembering school: mapping continuities in power, subjectivity & emotion in stories of school life*. Oxford: Peter Lang.

Starnes, B. and Paris, C. (2000). Choosing to Learn. *Phi Delta Kappan*, 81 (5), p. 392.

Stobart, G. (2014). *Expert learner*. London: McGraw-Hill Education.

Strand, S. (2014). Ethnicity, Gender, Social Class and Underachievement Gaps at Age 16: Intersectionality and 'Getting it' for the White Working Class. *Research Papers in Education*, 29, pp. 131–71.

Streib, J. (2011). Class Reproduction by Four Year Olds. *Qualitative Sociology*, 34, pp. 337–97.

Sullivan, A. (2002). Bourdieu and Education: How Useful is Bourdieu's Theory for Researchers?. *Netherlands Journal of Social Sciences*, 38 (2), pp. 144–66.

Sullivan, A. (2007). Cultural Capital, Cultural Knowledge and Ability. *Sociological Research Online*, 12 (6), pp. 1.

Sullivan, A., Parsons, S., Wiggins, R., Heath, A. and Green, F. (2014). Social Origins, School Type and Higher Education Destinations. *Oxford Review of Education*, 40 (6), pp. 739–63.

Thornberg, R. (2008). 'It's Not Fair!' – Voicing Pupils' Criticisms of School Rules. *Children and Society*, 22, pp. 418–28.

Torrance, H. (2012). Formative Assessment at the Crossroads: Conformative, Deformative and Transformative Assessment. *Oxford Review of Education*, 38 (3), pp. 323–42.

Torrance, H. and Pryor, J. (1998). *Investigating formative assessment: Teaching, learning and assessment in the classroom*. Maidenhead: McGraw-Hill Education.

UKCES (2012) *Why businesses should recruit young people*. Briefing paper, available online at www.ukces.org.uk/assets/ukces/docs/publications/why-businesses-should-recruit-young people.pdf (accessed 21 Feb. 2017).

UNCRC-United Nations (1989). *Convention on the Rights of the Child*. New York: UNICEF.

Unger, R. (2011). The Future of the Left. *The European*.

Vygotsky, L.S. (1962). *Language and thought*. Ontario: Massachusetts Institute of Technology Press.

Watkins, C. (2001). Learning About Learning Enhances Performance. *INSI Research Matters*, 13, pp. 1–9.

Watkins, C. (2005). *Classrooms as learning communities*. Oxford: Routledge.

Watkins, C. (2013). Forget Everything and Run. *School Leadership Today*, 4 (6), 27–30.

Watkins, C. (2015). Metalearning in Classrooms. In: D. Scott and E. Hargreaves, eds, *The SAGE handbook of learning*. London: Sage, pp. 321–30.

Watkins, C. (2010). Learning, Performance and Improvement. *INSI Research Matters*, Summer 2010 (34), pp. 1–16.

Watkins, C. (2016). Chriswatkins.net, a resource for learning. Available at http://chriswatkins.net (accessed 26 Sept. 2016).

Watkins, C., Carnell, E. and Lodge, C. (2007). *Effective learning in classrooms*. London: Paul Chapman.

Weber, M. (1958). The Three Types of Legitimate Rule. *Berkeley Publications in Society and Institutions*, 4 (1), pp. 1–11.

Wells, G. (2000). Dialogic Inquiry in Education: Building on the Legacy of Vygotsky. In: C.D. Lee, ed., *Vygotskian perspectives on literacy research*. Cambridge: Cambridge University Press, pp. 51–85.

Williams, S.R. and Ivey, K.M. (2001). Affective Assessment and Mathematics Classroom Engagement: A Case Study. *Educational Studies in Mathematics*, 47 (1), pp. 75–100.

Yeomans, C. (2013). *Students' choice in learning*. MA dissertation, UCL Institute of Education.

Index

'ability' groups, 7, 113–120
Affouneh, S., 36
agency, 13
anger, 28–30, 37, 38, 90–91
anxiety, 90–91
authoritarianism
  autonomy and, 44–50, 54
  Bloom and, 124–125
  children's experiences of, 4–5, 28–30
  children's fear and, 31–40, *34*
  children's resistance to, 5, 44–48
  definitions of, 13–14, 40–43
  effects of, 23–28
  freedom versus prescription and, 48–50
  reasons for, 43–44
  structures of classrooms and, 3, 30–31
  teacher's feedback and, 82
authority
  autonomy and, 51–52, 54
  children's experiences of, 4–5, 19
  definitions of, 40–43
  effects of, 2, 23–24
  freedom versus prescription and, 48–50
autonomy
  authoritarianism and, 44–50, 54
  authority and, 51–52, 54
  choice and, 73–80
  collaboration and relatedness and, 5–6, 56–57,
    66–73, *70*
  definitions and concept of, 52–60
  distributed authority and, 2
  fear and, 63–66
  metalearning and, 61–66, *62*, 77–80
  teacher's feedback and, 7, 57, 82, 84–86,
    87–89, 98, 101

Barbeau, E., 107
Bernstein, B., 21–22, 121
Black, P., 83
Bloom, A., 8, 124–125
Boaler, J., 114
Booth, S.A., 17
Boudon, R., 121

Bourdieu, P., 120–121
Bow Group, 106
Brown, A., 2
Bruner, J., 55
Burke, C., 10–11, 111

Campbell, T., 113
Caron, C., 49
Chavs (Jones), 108–109
children's experiences of classrooms
  cognitive, affective, social and physical aspects
    of, 17–19
  as different from adult's perceptions, 15–17
  importance of, 1–3, 10–15, 20
children's rights, 14–15
choice, 73–80
Christian religion, 25–26, 43
The Class (Entre Les Murs) (film), 20
Cognitive Evaluation Theory (CET), 54
collaboration, 56–57, 66–73, *70*, 102–103
collaborative group learning (CGL), 69–73, *70*
collectionist, 21, 41, 86
competence, 5–6, 53–54, 76–77, 84–85, 117,
    119–120
confusion, 90–91, 93–98
constructivism, 43
convergent feedback, 57, 83
critical inquiry, 7, 56, 57, 59, 88, 89, 102
critical reflection, 13, 22, 52, 55–56, 58
Crossouard, B., 57–58, 69, 83
cultural capital, 120–121

Deci, E.L., 51, 53–54, 55, 61, 66–67, 84
descriptive feedback, 83, 88
Devine, D., 14, 26–27, 109–110, 114
Dewey, J.
  on autonomy, 14, 51, 56–57, 58, 61, 66
  on creativity, 26
  on freedom, 48
  on schooling and learning, 11
  on self-direction, 13
directive feedback, 83, 87, 98–104
distributed authority, 2–3, 13, 20, 24, 25

distributed expertise, 2
divergent feedback, 83
Dweck, C.S., 62, 99, 102

Edwards, A., 18
effort, 116–118, 119–120
Egypt, 8, 16–17, 59–60
embarrassment, 90–91
Emerald Primary School, 3, 8, 59, 81, 87–98
Entre Les Murs (The Class) (film), 20
ethnic minority groups, 107–108
evaluative feedback, 83, 84, 88
experience, 17–19
exploratory feedback (provocative feedback), 57,
    83, 90, 99

facilitative feedback, 99–104
fear, 4–5, 31–40, *34*, 63–66, 90–91
Fielding, M., 12, 49, 57, 124–125
Filer, J., 9, 77–80
Fisher, H., 48, 59, 92
fixed mindset (performance orientation),
    117–118
Foucault, M., 26, 30–31, 47
Francis, B., 114
freedom, 48–50
The Freedom Writers (film), 123
Freire, P., 13–14, 24, 26, 48–50, 54–55
frustration, 90–91

Gamoran, A., 114–115
Garg, S., 9, 30
Gipps, C., 83, 84, 88
Giroux, H., 43
governmentality, 47
Gratton, R., 9, 69–73, *70*
Green, A., 120
Grosvenor, I., 10–11, 111
growth mindset (learning orientation), 62, 99,
    102, 117–118
Gruwell, E., 8, 122–124

Hallam, S., 115
Harber, C., 4, 14, 24, 25, 42
Haroon, S., 9, 27–28
Hattie, J., 83–84, 88
help-seeking, 119
Heneghan, H., 9, 28–29
Holt, J., 31–32, 34, 42
Hopkins, E., 11
hostility, 90–91
human capital, 107
human rights, 14–15
humour, 87, 92

Illeris, K., 85–86, 90
in-work poverty, 107

inequality, 121
initiation response feedback (IRF) cycle,
    57, 82
integrationist approach, 22, 41

Jackson, C., 27
James, M., 86
Jones, O., 108–109
Ju, W., 9, 108

Karvela, K., 9, 29
Kemmis, S., 58
knowledge of results (KR), 82
Kohn, A., 13, 55

learner-centred ideology, 22, 122
learning, 2, 3, 5, 6, 11, 12, 13, 15–19, 21–22, 28,
    31–33, 36, 39–40, 49, 52–55, 61–62, 67,
    69–72, 74–77, 78–79, 83–84, 91–92, 99,
    102–3, 115, 117, 119, 122, 125
learning journals, 61
Lefstein, A., 30–31
legitimate authority, 40–41
Lin, A.M., 82
linguistic domination, 121
Little, D., 52

Macedonia, 17
Macfarlane-Dick, D., 101
MacInnes, T., 107
MacIntyre, D., 13
Macleod, G., 24
Macnamara, S., 9, 113, 115–120, 124
Marton, F., 17
McCallum, B., 59
McGillicuddy, D., 14
Meadowbank Primary School, 4–5, 8, 24,
    32–36, 63, 67–69
Meighan, R., 25, 42
Mesirow, J., 19
metacognition, 62
metalearning, 6, 39–40, 61–62, *62*, 77–80
metasocial critical inquiry, 88, 89
Moore, A., 16, 18, 28, 92

Nandy, L., 120
Nash, P., 25, 49
nervousness, 90–91
new authoritarianism, 43
Nicol, D.J., 101
Noddings, N., 15
Nordlander, E., 111

Opdenakker, M., 28, 109
oppression, 13–14, 121
Organisation for Economic Co-operation and
    Development (OECD), 106

Palestine, 8, 36–40
Parsons, S., 115
Passeron, J.-C., 120–121
peer-led feedback, 103–104
peer pressure, 118–119
Perrenoud, P., 86
phenomenography, 17–19
Piaget, J., 15, 16, 55
Plato, 14
Pratt, N., 43
proactivity, 87, 89
process-focused feedback, 83–84
provocative feedback (exploratory feedback), 57,
    83, 90, 99. *See also* faciliative feedback
Pryor, J., 57–58, 81, 83
punishments, 26, 27–28, 34

Quick, L., 5, 9, 24, 44–49, 53

Raby, R., 49
Read Write Inc. (RWI), 98–104
Reay, D., 8, 105, 108, 109, 110, 111–113, 114
relatedness, 5–6, 53, 66–73, *70*, 85, 102, 114,
    123–124
relational experience, 18
religion, 25–26, 43
resilience, 117–118
Rogers, C., 25
Rolls, L., 9, 98–104
Romanish, B., 44
Ruddock, J., 49
Ryan, R.M., 51, 53–54, 61, 66–67, 84

Saevi, T., 18, 19
Schiro, M., 20–22, 31, 106, 111, 120–121
scholar academics, 21
schooling, purposes of, 21–22, 120–122
self-determination theory, 53–54, 61, 66–67, 84
self-direction, 13, 101–102
self-regulation-focused feedback, 83–84
self-regulatory feedback, 103–104
self-related feedback, 84–86, 88
silence, 15, 30, 36, 37
silencing, 2, 4, 6, 12, 20, 43, 110
singularity, 87, 89
social class
    'ability' groups and, 113–120
    Bloom and, 124–125
    children's views of, 7–8, 111–112
    in the classroom, 108–111

social class *cont.*
    cultural capital and, 120–121
    definitions of working class, 107–108
    Schiro's purposes of schooling and, 120–122
    school as segregated system and, 105–107
    social justice and, 122–124
social efficiency ideology, 21, 122
social justice, 122–124
social power, 58
social reconstruction ideology, 22, 122
soft skills, 107
Son, Y. J., 9, 29
Southgate, E., 26, 35
stereotypes, 110
Stobart, G., 113
Strand, S., 106
stress, 28–30
student voice, 12–13
Sullivan, A., 106, 120, 121
surveillance, 30–31

teacher's feedback
    autonomy and, 7, 57, 82, 84–86, 87–89,
        98, 101
    children's critique of directive feedback and,
        98–104
    children's responses to, 3, 6–7, 87–92
    definitions and concept of, 81–86
    teachers' and children's purposes and, 93–98
Thornberg, R., 42
Timperly, H., 83–84, 88
Torrance, H., 57, 58, 81, 83
transformative learning, 19

unconditional positive regard, 25

Van Damme, J., 28, 109
voice, 12–13
Vygotsky, L., 3, 55, 72

Watkins, C., 61, 62, 117
Weber, M., 41
well-being, 75–76
Wiliam, D., 83
working class, definitions of, 107–108. *See also*
    social class

Yeomans, C., 9, 73–77

zones of proximal development, 72